Sharon L. Vanderlip, D.V.M.

Scottish Terriers

Everything About History, Care,
Nutrition, Handling, and Behavior

Filled with Full-color Photographs
and Illustrations

BARRON'S

²CONTENTS

3

SCOTTISH TERRIER HISTORY

The origin of the Scottish Terrier forever will remain a mystery lost in time, for it is true that the older the dog breed, the less recorded history there is available. Of all the dog breeds we know today, the Scottish Terrier is one of the oldest and most primitive on earth. It is also one of the purest of breeds, maintaining its distinctive type and character throughout the ages.

Origin of the Breed

Although we do not know all the details of the breed's history, we do know that the Scottish Terrier has been a valued friend of man for centuries. Literary works and paintings from long ago vividly portray the same robust, courageous, and dignified dog that typifies the Scottish Terrier we admire today.

History's Mystery

Much of the history of the breed is speculative. In fact, one early author seriously suggested (incorrectly) that the Scottish Terrier was descended from bears, rather than ancient canines! In spite of the many unanswered questions about the breed's past, it is widely accepted that the Scottish Terrier is the original and most ancient terrier breed of the

Dignified, brave, and intelligent, the Scottish Terrier is recognized and loved worldwide.

Scottish Highlands. Throughout its history, the Scottish Terrier was known by a variety of names, including the Aberdeen, the Highland Terrier, the Die-hard, the Scotch Terrier, the Fox Terrier, the Otter Dog, the West Highland Terrier, the Cairn Terrier, and the Skye Terrier. These names were derived from areas where the Scottish Terrier could be found or from the prey it hunted, as well as from its bold and tenacious behavior (Die-hard).

Most of today's dog fanciers and historians agree that other Highland terrier breeds, such as the Skye Terrier and the West Highland White Terrier, are descendents of the Scottish Terrier. It is important to mention that even though the Scottish Terrier was sometimes called a Skye or Cairn Terrier, it did not look like the Skye and Cairn Terriers we recognize today as separate and distinct breeds, distantly related to the Scottish Terrier.

From the earliest times, Scottish Terriers proved themselves to be wonderful companions, excellent guardians, and hard workers. Bold, strong, fearless, and determined, the Scottish Terrier's ability to seek out and kill rodents and small game made it a valuable addition to the highland country home. In each glen, people developed individual strains of Highland Terriers with characteristics that suited their particular hunting needs.

Held in High Regard

Admired, respected, and loved for its loyalty, spirit, and bravery, the Scottish Terrier was held in high regard by everyone from country peasants to royalty. They were so valued that in the 17th century, King James VI of Scotland, who later became James I of England, sent six terriers to France as a royal gift.

In 1860 the first Scottish Terrier class was offered at a dog show in Birmingham, England.

Other dog shows followed suit and dogs purported to be Scottish Terriers were subsequently exhibited. The problem was, there were various types of terriers exhibited and many did not resemble what the populace of the time considered to be the original Scottish Terrier. As you might expect, dog fanciers protested. In 1877 they filed a series of letters in the *Live Stock Journal*, arguing the various points and characteristics of the true Scottish Terrier. The editor of the *Live Stock Journal* responded by asking readers to provide a description of what they considered to be the correct Scottish Terrier type. Captain Gordon Murray, a terrier aficionado, took up the challenge, under the pen name of "Strathbogie," and submitted his version of the ideal Scottish Terrier. Everyone seemed to agree with his description, so in 1880 James B. Morrison outlined the standard for the breed in the *Live Stock Journal*. Later he and D.J. Thomson Gray drew up the first official Scottish Terrier standard. So solid was the standard that only minor changes have been made to it since that time.

In 1882 the first Scottish Terrier club was formed, with James B. Morrison as president and D. J. Thomson Gray as vice-president. Soon after, in 1883, John Naylor, a Scottish immigrant, imported the first Scottish Terriers to the United States. His first imports were a

The Scottish Terrier is anatomically designed for power and endurance.

pair named Tam Glen and Bonnie Bell. His later imports included Glenlyon and Whinstone. Glenlyon sired the first Scottish Terrier born in America (whelped September 15, 1884). The first Scottish Terrier to be registered by the American Kennel Club (AKC) was Prince Charlie, number 3310, in 1885.

The Scottish Terrier Club of America was formed in 1900 under the leadership of Dr. Fayette Ewing. And so the most ancient and pure of terrier breeds was simultaneously introduced to the United States and launched into the 20th century.

American Kennel Club Group Classifications

Group I	Sporting Dogs
Group II	Hounds
Group III	Working Dogs
Group IV	Terriers
Group V	Toys
Group VI	Non-Sporting Dogs
Group VII	Herding Dogs
Miscellaneous class	

Today's Scottish Terrier Standard

In 1993 the American Kennel Club approved the Scottish Terrier Club of America's Standard of Points. The complete standard may be obtained from the AKC.

Appearance

In essence, the standard for the Scottish Terrier has changed little since James B. Morrison outlined the first standard in 1880. The Scottish Terrier's small, compact, short-legged, sturdily-built confirmation remains a trademark of the breed. The Scottish Terrier is a dog of substance. Its head is long in proportion to its size. In profile, the skull appears flat and the skull and muzzle give the appearance of two parallel planes, with a slight, but definite stop between the skull and muzzle at eye level. The eyes are almond-shaped, dark brown in color, and set in under the brow. The muzzle is approximately equal to the length of skull with a slight taper to the large, black nose. The Scottish Terrier's body is moderately short with a deep, broad chest and very muscular hindquarters. The topline of the back is firm and level. The ears and tail are carried erect, giving the dog a keen, alert appearance. Although dew claws may be removed, the tail is never cut. It is normally about 7 inches (17 cm) in length. The broken outer coat of the adult is harsh, wiry (but not curly), and weather-resistant. Pups may have softer, even silky coats, but the harsh coat eventually replaces the puppy coat. The adult undercoat is soft and dense, to protect against inclement weather. In the early days of the breed, Scottish Terriers were found in gray, wheaten, brindle, and red-brindle, but not black. Today, acceptable colors include black. Sprinklings of white or silver hairs are normal, with an occasional dash of white on the chest or chin.

Scottish Terriers are about 10 inches (25 cm) tall at the withers when they are full grown. Males weigh between 19 and 22 pounds (8.6–10 kg) and females between 18 and 21 pounds (8.2–9.5 kg).

The Scottish Terrier is a hardy, adaptable, and bold breed.

The Scottish Terrier ranks among the top ten most popular terrier breeds.

A Scottish Terrier visits Franklin D. Roosevelt's historical office, sitting where the beloved and famous "Fala" once sat, more than a half-century ago.

Scottish Terriers are born with their ears folded. As they grow, their ears eventually become erect.

A brindle, wheaton, and black Scottish Terrier share a photo op.

Sometimes mother doesn't feel like playing. Without its littermates, a lone pup can become bored. Now is a good time to cheer up a brooding pup.

Group IV: Terriers

Airedale Terrier	
American Staffordshire Terrier	Manchester Terrier
Australian Terrier	Miniature Bull Terrier
Bedlington Terrier	Miniature Schnauzer
Border Terrier	Norfolk Terrier
Bull Terrier	Norwich Terrier
Cairn Terrier	Scottish Terrier
Dandie Dinmont Terrier	Sealyham Terrier
Fox Terrier, Smooth	Skye Terrier
Fox Terrier, Wire	Soft Coated Wheaten Terrier
Irish Terrier	Staffordshire Bull Terrier
Kerry Blue Terrier	Welsh Terrier
Lakeland Terrier	West Highland White Terrier

The Scottish Terrier is confident and bold, with a dignity that commands respect. It is no wonder it is fondly referred to as "power in a small package."

The Scottish Terrier's Place in the Dog World

The Scottish Terrier is a member of the Terrier group (AKC classification Group IV), which consists of several breeds of dogs that were bred to hunt and kill pests and vermin and to protect the farm and family. Although terriers may range in size, they are all courageous and feisty. The smaller terrier breeds are as bold and fearless as their larger cousins. Terriers are renowned for their busy, outgoing, and investigative nature, and especially for their tenaciousness.

Popularity

Of the 148 breeds currently recognized by the AKC, the Scottish Terrier continues to rank among the top 50 in number of dogs registered, with 4,369 Scottish Terriers registered in 1999 alone. *Dogs USA Annual* lists the Scottish Terrier in an impressive third place among the top ten most popular terrier breeds of the new millennium!

Scottish Terrier Celebrities

Every Scottish Terrier is a celebrity in its own right. This becomes evident from the first time you take your pet out for a walk and are surrounded by admirers. In spite of the fact that the Scottish Terrier is not a common breed, its

Scotty Recap

✔ Scottish Terriers are the original and most ancient terrier breed of the Scottish Highlands.

✔ Scottish Terriers have been known by a variety of names, including the Aberdeen, the Highland Terrier, the Die-hard, the Scotch Terrier, the Fox Terrier, the Otter Dog, the West Highland Terrier, the Cairn Terrier, and the Skye Terrier.

✔ Scottish Terriers earned their reputations as excellent guardians and hard workers.

✔ They have a keen ability to seek out and kill rodents and small game.

✔ The first Scottish Terrier class was offered at a dog show in England in 1860.

✔ The first Scottish Terrier club was formed in 1882, and soon thereafter, the first Scottish Terrier was imported to the United States.

✔ The Scottish Terrier Club of America was formed in 1900.

✔ The Scottish Terrier continues to rank among the top 50 of the 148 breeds currently recognized by the AKC, in the number of dogs registered.

✔ The Scottish Terrier has been listed in third place among the top ten most popular terrier breeds of the new millennium.

endearing personage is recognized worldwide and immediately associated with its homeland. Advertisers of Scotch whiskey have used the Scottish Terrier's fame to their advantage for promotional purposes and President Franklin D. Roosevelt's Scottish Terrier, Fala, did more than his share to draw attention to his breed and make "Scottish Terrier" a household phrase.

Among some of the more famous Scottish Terriers is Champion Braeburn's Close Encounter, the breed's top winner with more than two hundred Best in Show titles.

Countless other Scottish Terriers have earned their place in the spotlight, in the show ring, in the obedience ring, in military service, and in community service. But any Scottish Terrier owner can tell you that the biggest celebrity of all is the pet Scottish Terrier. "Scotty" and "Annie" earn their reputations and status daily by being constant and loyal companions, protecting their loved ones, and securing a place in the heart forever.

CONSIDERATIONS BEFORE YOU BUY

Now that you have fallen in love with the breed, you must be certain that a Scottish Terrier is the right dog for you. After all, you will be sharing the next ten or more years with your new companion, so you want to be sure that your lifestyles and personalities are compatible.

Is a Scottish Terrier the Right Dog for You?

Every Scottish Terrier has its own unique personality, but there are distinct behavioral and genetic (inherited) traits characteristic of the breed that are deeply engrained in these independent little dogs—characteristics that have made it possible for the breed to survive the harsh conditions of its native land. These include a robust and muscular body to enable it to climb steep, craggy, hills and terrain; large feet and nose, making it easy to detect small animals and quickly dig them out of hiding; powerful jaws to grasp, shake, and tear prey; and a harsh coat to repel the rain and provide warmth in a harsh climate. This sturdy dog is no pushover and will not be intimidated.

It's easy to fall in love with a Scottish Terrier. But before you buy, be sure that you are ready to make a long-term commitment to provide the care and love this remarkable canine deserves!

The Commitment

Whether to bring a new dog into your life, and when to do it, are major decisions that require serious consideration before you take action. Dog ownership, or guardianship, as many people now refer to it, is not only a joy—it is also a serious responsibility. During the years, your companion will rely on you for love, attention, proper nutrition, training, and good health care. To satisfy these requirements, you must be prepared not only for the financial aspects of responsible pet ownership, but also for the investments you cannot really measure: time and emotion.

If you have made your decision and your heart is set on a Scottish Terrier, here are some considerations to help you choose the best time to introduce a new Scottish Terrier into your life and your home.

The Best Time to Acquire a Scottish Terrier

Although you may want a Scottish Terrier right now, today might not be the best time to buy your pet. With the Scottish Terrier's continual popularity, it may be difficult to find one immediately. Start contacting breeders immediately so you can be on their waiting list. Sometimes it's hard to be patient, but in the end you will find a Scottish Terrier of the age, sex, and temperament you want and you won't be disappointed.

If you have obligations and your free time is limited, you should postpone obtaining a dog until you will have the time to give the care and attention all dogs deserve. Scottish Terriers are bright and active. They become bored when left alone for long periods of time, especially when they are pups. A bored dog is prone to mischief. With no one to keep it company and nothing to do, any dog of any breed can develop unwanted behaviors, including barking, chewing, digging, and destroying.

If you are moving or changing jobs, a new pet can add stress rather than enjoyment. If you are planning a vacation soon, you will have to make arrangements for animal care in your absence. Rather than stress your new companion by a change in environment and caregivers, it is probably best to wait until you return from vacation before you introduce a new dog into your home.

Holidays: We all have seen the movies, animations, and advertisements in which a young puppy is wrapped up in bows sitting by the fireplace as a surprise holiday gift. There are two things very wrong with this concept. First, it is unwise to buy a pet for someone else. Pet ownership is a responsibility not everyone wants to assume. Second, adding a new pet to the family during the holiday season should be discouraged. This is a time when most people already have plenty to do with visitors and commitments. A new dog can be overlooked in the busy shuffle with all the distractions and excitement. Families do not have time to learn about, supervise, socialize, and care for a new animal during the holidays. Visitors and guests may stress, frighten, or mishandle the new dog. They may even be bitten. Someone may forget

It is natural for your Scottish Terrier to want to dig. It is up to you to teach your pet which areas are off-limits.

Scottish Terriers need lots of love, attention, and training. Before you add one to your family, be sure that you have enough free time to enjoy and care for your new companion.

to close the crate, a door, or a fence gate and your new friend may escape, be lost or injured, or killed by a moving vehicle. In the holiday confusion, an animal can be overfed or miss a meal, unless someone is specifically assigned the responsibility of feeding. Finally, dogs purchased and transported (especially in cold weather) during the holidays may prone to more stress or illness than usual.

Household Pets

Your Scottish Terrier ("Annie") is bold and fiercely curious. She has a keen sense of smell and is interested in meeting all the new members of your family, including other household

Is a Scotty Right for You?

Here's a little quiz to help you determine if a Scottish Terrier is the right dog for you.

1 Do you enjoy the company of a dog that will stand its ground, yet is gentle in nature?

2 Do you appreciate the qualities of an animal that is courageous and loyal, yet often a "one-owner dog," tending to form a close bond with one family member? (This special person is not necessarily the one who feeds the dog!)

3 Can you relate to a dog that may appear aloof at times, if you know that it is actually assessing a situation and will form its relationships (with people or other pets) at its own pace?

4 Do you have the patience for a dog that definitely has a mind of its own and is not only alert and appealing, but also is very intelligent—sometimes to the point that it may, at times, appear to be stubborn?

5 Can you forgive your dog for behaviors that may be unacceptable in today's modern world (for example, digging holes in the flower garden or lawn to hunt out prey), but that have evolved over centuries as a mechanism to ensure the breed's very survival?

If you have answered these questions with a positive response, then you just might be ready to join the ranks of thousands of people who have owned and loved Scottish Terriers!

The Scottish Terrier is robust and muscular. Its large nose is a key asset in helping it hunt and find small prey.

A beautifully groomed, well-mannered Scottish Terrier is a pleasure to photograph, in any setting.

pets. Make sure the introductions are done slowly and safely. For example, if you own another dog or a cat, don't expect them to be friends at the onset. Your other pets will be cautious and possibly jealous of the newcomer. A resentful cat can inflict serious injury on an unsuspecting puppy. Eye injuries from cat scratches are not uncommon accidents experienced by dogs. And if you have another dog in the home, remember that the dog may be jealous of the attention you are bestowing on

Annie, particularly if your dog is an adult or aged animal. Even if your pets are happy to have Annie join the family, be sure that they do not play too roughly and accidentally injure her.

A good way to start introductions in the family is to place Annie in an area of the home where she is safe from other animals, but where they can observe and smell each other. For example, if you have a laundry area, or a space off the kitchen, you can place a baby

Your new puppy will miss its mother and littermates. If you give it the love and attention it deserves, it won't be lonely.

barrier gate to prevent the new arrival from running loose in the house without your permission, until she adapts to her new environment and your other pets are used to her. You may also put Annie in her crate the first few evenings so that your other household animals can approach and investigate, but not harm her. Remember to pay extra attention to your established pets so they are not jealous.

A healthy Scottish Terrier puppy is active and mischievous. Be sure to provide lots of safe toys to keep your pet busy and out of harm's way.

Scottish Terriers are natural hunters. Be sure all of your household pets are safely isolated from your dog.

Note: In most cases, animals learn to live together in a household peacefully. However, there are some household pets Annie should never meet. These include any small mammals (such as hamsters, rabbits, guinea pigs, or ferrets), birds, or reptiles. Instinct will tell Annie that these small animals should be hunted out and killed immediately. Even a Scottish Terrier puppy has a strong instinct to dig out and destroy small prey! Small pets and birds sense when there is a predator in the area. They will be frightened and stressed if their cage is approached. Scottish Terriers are very clever, so make sure the lid or door to your small pet's cage is securely fastened. Then place the cage where Annie cannot find it. Remember, she has a very keen sense of smell and will easily find

these animals, so don't just place them out of sight—make sure they are out of reach!

Should Your Scottish Terrier Be Neutered?

Scottish Terriers are hardy dogs that do extremely well with tender loving care, exercise, proper nutrition, and preventive veterinary care. One of the most important health decisions you will make is whether to have Annie spayed, or, if you have a male Scottish Terrier ("Scotty"), to have him castrated. These procedures (called "neutering") refer to the inactivation or removal of some, or all, of the tissues in the body associated with reproduction (testicles in the male, ovaries and uterus in the

Have your Scottish Terrier examined by a veterinarian within 48 hours of purchase. Your veterinarian can answer your questions and advise you on the many benefits of early spay and neuter.

female). Neutering is most often accomplished surgically, although there are also chemical methods that may become more commonplace in the future.

The Benefits

Early neutering can be safely performed on pups between six and sixteen weeks of age. Studies have shown that prepubertal gonadectomy does not affect growth rate, food intake, or weight gain of growing dogs. In 1993 the American Veterinary Medical Association formally approved of early neutering in the dog (and cat), a procedure many veterinarians and humane organizations have been promoting for years.

There are distinct health advantages for dogs that are neutered early in life:

✔ Significantly reduces the chance of developing mammary (breast) cancer if the ovaries are removed before the female's second, and preferably first, estrous cycle;

✔ Prevents ovarian, uterine, testicular, or epididymal diseases, such as cancer and infection;

✔ Prevents unwanted pregnancies;

✔ Requires less surgical procedure time;

✔ Allows for a rapid recovery period (Young, healthy animals heal quickly.)

✔ Leads to fewer behavior problems;

✔ Eliminates the inconveniences associated with a female dog in estrus (vaginal bleeding and discharge that can stain furniture and carpets and attract neighborhood dogs).

No procedure is completely without risk or side effects, so you should discuss all aspects of surgery with your veterinarian. However, rest assured that surgical neutering is successfully performed on healthy animals every day. Your veterinarian can advise you about the specific pros and cons of neutering.

SELECTING YOUR SCOTTISH TERRIER

The best way to find a Scottish Terrier is to begin with your local or national breed association. These associations will be able to provide a list of reputable Scottish Terrier breeders.

Where to Find a Scottish Terrier

You may also join a breed, or all-breed, dog club in your area where you can meet breeders, dog trainers, and professional dog show handlers who can provide a wealth of information about various breeders. Dog publications, available from your local bookstore or pet store, contain numerous advertisements placed by dog breeders with animals for sale.

Be sure to purchase from a reputable breeder. Don't be surprised if the breeder you select does not have puppies immediately available. Just remember that a good Scottish Terrier is well worth the wait. If you are certain you want to be the proud owner of a Scottish Terrier, it is not too early to start checking with breeders today.

A Scottish Terrier puppy is the ultimate Thief of Hearts!

Puppy or Adult?

Most people want to start with a puppy and there are many advantages to this approach. When purchasing any dog, the most important considerations are the animal's health, temperament, and personality. A dog's personality is well-established by the time it is eight to twelve weeks of age. By obtaining Scotty in the very early stages of life, you may positively influence his adult personality and behavior development. This is much easier than trying to change an established undesirable behavior in an adult dog. However, sometimes, for a variety of reasons, a breeder may have an adolescent or young adult dog available for sale. If the dog has been well-socialized as a youngster and well-trained, there are many advantages to purchasing an older dog. You can skip the trials and tribulations of puppyhood, including housebreaking, leash-training, and basic discipline (such as training your pet not to chew your belongings or dig in your garden). You must be certain, however, that you and the dog are a good match. It is not unreasonable to request a brief trial period when you purchase an adult dog, so that you can be sure the animal will adapt successfully to a new family and change of lifestyle.

An older, well-trained Scottish Terrier may be more expensive than a puppy. This is because a lot more time, effort, and expense have gone into the adult animal. Dog breeders often take a monetary loss on the sale of their animals. They raise dogs as a hobby, not as a source of income. The price you pay for Scotty will be insignificant compared to the costs you will incur in feeding, grooming supplies, toys, housing, and veterinary care during his life. These costs will far exceed his initial purchase price.

Selecting a Puppy

Once you have decided to buy a puppy and have located a breeder with animals available for sale, make an appointment to visit the breeder and see the puppies in person. Be sure to verify that Scotty has been registered and ask for a copy of his parents' registration papers. The breeder can also provide you with a copy of Scotty's pedigree. Ask the breeder if Scotty's parents have additional certifications, for example, registration by the Canine Eye Registration Foundation (CERF), or any type of testing for freedom of inherited health problems.

Watch Scotty in his home environment. Is he happy and outgoing? Is he alert and feisty? Is he playful and bold? Carefully observe Scotty and his littermates for signs of good health and strong personalities. A Scottish Terrier should not be timid or shy, but his instincts may warn him to be initially cautious. After Scotty has had an opportunity to investigate and get to know you, he should not be hesitant to approach and interact with you. Of course, you do not want a puppy that is too rambunctious or obnoxious, either. A good Scottish Terrier puppy is happy and courageous, but not overbearing or aggressive.

Next, check Scotty's eyes, ears, mouth, skin, coat, and movement. Are the eyes clear and

Puppy Health Checklist

Attitude	Healthy, alert, playful, inquisitive.
Eyes	Bright, clear, free of discharge.
Ears	Clean, free of dirt and wax buildup, no evidence of head-shaking or scratching.
Mouth	Gums bright pink, teeth properly aligned.
Skin and coat	Healthy, no evidence of parasites or sores; Scottish Terrier pups normally have a softer coat than adults.
Body condition	May seem a little plump, but should not have a distended belly or thin body.
Movement	Normal gait for a puppy; may seem a bit bouncy and sometimes clumsy.

bright? Are the ears clean? Are the gums bright pink and are the teeth properly aligned? Are the skin and coat healthy and free of parasites or sores? Are the hindquarters and under the tail clean, with no signs of blood or diarrhea? Does Scotty run and play in a normal manner?

Finally, ask to see and handle both parents, if they are available. This will help you determine their personalities and give you a good idea of how you might expect Scotty to behave when he is an adult. Remember, however, that the way you raise and handle him will have a big influence on his character and temperament.

Male or Female?

If you are looking for a wonderful companion that will keep you entertained and be a faithful guardian, then either a male or female Scottish Terrier will do very well.

If you are thinking of raising Scottish Terriers in the future, then you should seriously consider your options and discuss these plans with the breeder, who can assist you in making an appropriate decision on which animal to purchase at the onset. Most novice breeders begin by investing in the best female they can find, often an adult that has proven herself in the show ring and/or previously produced a litter. Then, with the help of an experienced breeder, the novice finds the most suitable stud dog for the female and pays for its services.

If you do not plan to breed Scottish Terriers, you should definitely have your dog, male or female, neutered as early as possible, for reasons previously discussed.

When considering size, remember that both the male and female Scottish Terriers measure about 10 inches (25 cm) at the withers, although the males are slightly heavier at 19 to 22 pounds (8.6–10 kg), females weighing 18 to 21 pounds (8.2–9.5 kg).

Age and Longevity

It is a fact that small dog breeds live longer than large breeds, and the Scottish Terrier is no exception. Scottish Terriers are hardy dogs and with good nutrition and loving care they can live more than 12 years. This is another reason why you should be particular when choosing your companion. Dog guardianship is a long-term commitment!

Registering Your Scottish Terrier

One of the many pleasures of owning a purebred dog is pride of ownership and the variety of activities in which you and your companion can participate. For example, without registration papers, there is no proof of parentage or lineage. When you purchase Scotty, be sure to verify that both of his parents are registered and that he has been registered as well. Do not confuse official registration with a pedigree. A pedigree is a record of the animal's immediate family members (parents, grandparents, great-grandparents) that the breeder can provide you. Registration is an official document issued by the kennel club that is proof that a dog is purebred.

Deciding between a puppy or an adult is difficult! Both have so much to offer, you just might decide to buy one of each!

Scottish Terriers are born as good dogs with wonderful dispositions.

Scotties are inquisitive and bold—attributes that remain throughout their lives.

Obtain as much information as possible about your Scottish Terrier, before you buy it.

Scottish Terrier puppies have softer coats than adults.

Scottish Terriers must be registered with the AKC in order to participate in dog shows.

TIP

Questions to Ask

12 important questions to ask the seller:

1 Are the pups purebred and registered?

2 How old are the pups and what sexes are available?

3 At what age were the pups weaned?

4 How many pups were in the litter?

5 Have the pups received any inoculations? If so, which ones?

6 Have the pups been wormed or tested for worms?

7 Have the pups had their eyes examined by a veterinary ophthalmologist? If so, ask to see the eye certification.

8 Have the pups been handled frequently and are they socialized?

9 Have the pups received any basic training (housebreaking, leash-training)?

10 What kind of food are the pups eating at this time?

11 Can you have a 48-hour health guarantee until you can have the puppy examined by your own veterinarian?

12 Can you see the parents of the pups, and if you cannot see them, why not?

CHECKLIST

Selection Pointers

✔ Begin the search for your Scottish Terrier by contacting a local or national breed association.

✔ After locating a breeder or other appropriate seller, be certain to ask the 12 important questions listed above.

✔ When purchasing your Scottish Terrier, remember that the animal's health, tem-perament, and personality are the most important factors to consider.

✔ When deciding between a puppy or adult, remember that each has its advantages as well as disadvantages.

✔ When choosing a puppy, whether male or female, remember to have your Scottish Terrier neutered if you do not plan to breed your dog.

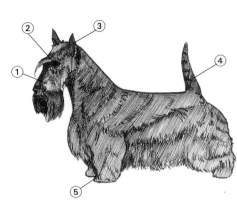

Illustrated Standard

1. Long skull, of medium width
2. Small, almond-shaped eyes
3. Prick ears, pointed
4. Uncut tail, about 7" long, carried with a slight curve but not over the back
5. Legs, short and heavy boned

❏ **Color:** black, wheaten, or brindle of any color
❏ **DQ:** none*

*DQ = disqualification

Scotty Quick Reference Chart

Listed below are some of the most important attributes that owners look at before purchasing a dog. Also listed are the rankings for the Scottish Terrier breed. Once you have decided that you want a Scotty, refer to this chart again and make certain that your requirements and needs match those of the breed.

	High	Moderate	Low
Grooming Needs		✔	
Trainability			✔
Watchdog Ability	✔		
Affection Level		✔	
Playfulness		✔	
Energy Level		✔	
Exercise Needs		✔	
Friendliness		✔	

AT HOME WITH YOUR SCOTTISH TERRIER

You have done your homework, found the perfect Scottish Terrier, and now you are eager to bring her home and make her feel comfortable and secure. Part of your pet's success in adapting to her new family and her new life depends on making sure you are well-prepared for the new arrival.

If you have everything ready in advance that you both will need, the transition period will go smoothly.

Your Scottish Terrier Comes Home

Ideally, your new acquisition will have been introduced to a travel kennel before you bring her home. A travel kennel makes an ideal portable doghouse for Scottish Terriers, so this is an item that you will use frequently, for travel and home. If Annie has a favorite toy or blanket, ask the seller if you can place it in the travel kennel for the trip home. A familiar item will help her feel more secure during the trip and during the next few days in her new environment.

Place the familiar item, or a soft blanket or towel, in the travel kennel on top of a layer of

Your Scottish Terrier should have no difficulty at all making itself right at home!

shredded newspaper. Make sure Annie has not eaten for the last two hours so that she is less likely to become carsick and doesn't vomit. The trip home may be the first time she has ever traveled in a car. If she feels queasy, she may drool excessively, so be sure to bring along plenty of paper towels. Allow Annie to relieve herself before you place her in the travel kennel.

Your new friend may protest all the way home, or she may simply sleep. Make a decision right now not to give in to her crying, no matter how difficult it is. Talk to her soothingly, but be forewarned! If you hold her on your lap for the trip home, she will not forget it, and will expect you to allow her on your lap every car trip you take together. When she is an adult she will be larger and stronger and heavier. It is safer for both of you if she remains in her travel kennel whenever she travels in the car.

The Arrival

When you arrive home, give Annie a small drink of water. Remember that she is probably

For the safety of your pet and everyone in the car, always transport your Scottish Terrier in a travel crate designed specifically for that pupose.

fatigued from her trip and all of the excitement, so a little quiet time is in order. If she is sleepy, allow her to rest. If she feels like becoming acquainted, do so calmly and gently. Avoid loud noises and sudden movements.

Children: Be sure to teach any children in the home to respect Annie's space and privacy. Teach them the proper way to lift and handle her, by gently putting one hand under the chest and the other under the hindquarters for support. Never lift a Scottish Terrier by the scruff of the neck or by the limbs. Small children should remain seated on the floor when petting or handling a puppy, to prevent dropping or injury.

Naming Your Scottish Terrier

The first thing your Scottish Terrier will need to learn is her name. Once she knows her name, you can get her attention and start a line of communication—the first step in her lifelong training.

Your dog's personality will shine through at the onset so you will most likely have no difficulty thinking of a name that suits your companion and her character. If you need some

ideas, you will find plenty in dog magazines and books of baby names. (We will use "Scotty" and "Annie".)

It seems easier for dogs to recognize names with two syllables. This avoids confusion later on when you give one-syllable commands, such as *sit, stay,* and *down.* Names ending in a vowel sound also are easy for dogs to identify, such as "Scotty" or "Anna." If you usually call your dog by its two-syllable name, do not shorten it later ("Scotty" to "Scot") or your dog can become confused.

When you have selected a name, use it often when talking to your new pet. When she responds or comes to you, praise her lavishly. It won't take her long to know who she is.

Housing Considerations

Scottish Terriers are extremely adaptable and although their hardy ancestors survived centuries of tough times and harsh conditions, today's Scottish Terriers prefer the same creature comforts you do, if given a choice. They enjoy living indoors as much as they love to play outside. The most important housing considerations are comfort, safety, and freedom from boredom. If bored or lonely, any dog will get into trouble and develop bad habits (barking, chewing, digging, and scratching).

Location

When you bring Annie home, decide on a safe place (an X-pen, laundry room, area off of the kitchen) where she can feel secure and have some privacy, yet be observed. Ideally, this area will be Annie's permanent housing and sleeping quarters. Take her to her new den to explore and relax for several minutes. Feed her a little treat and praise her. Annie should associate her space with enjoyment. It should be a pleasant place to be. Make sure she can also observe the household activities so she doesn't feel isolated. Scottish Terriers are intelligent, active dogs and they enjoy being a central part of everything going on around them. Exposure to various sights, sounds, smells, activities, and people are all an important part of socializing a dog. Remember that Annie doesn't know the rules yet and will require training, so make sure her den is in an area where she cannot chew furniture or urinate on the carpet. Later, when you have started training her, do not use her sleeping quarters as a place to go when she is punished. Her territory should always be a comforting place where she goes when all is right with the world, and not when she is in trouble.

If you have acquired an older Scottish Terrier, try to duplicate the previous housing situation as much as possible to reduce the stress of changing environments.

Safety First

Annie will be very curious and interested in learning more about her new home. Some of the characteristics you admire most about your dog—her intelligence, small size, and

Your Scottish Terrier enjoys all the creature comforts you do. Give your companion an area all its own that is clean, safe, warm, and comfortable.

TIP

Scotty Supplies

Supplies you will need for your new Scottish Terrier:

✔ Food and water dishes
✔ Quality puppy/dog food
✔ Comfortable sleeping quarters (dog bed, doghouse, designated area in home)
✔ Travel kennel
✔ Identification tag
✔ Collar
✔ Leash
✔ Grooming supplies (brush, comb, blunt-tipped scissors, nail trimmers, styptic powder, gentle emollient shampoo, ear cleaning solution)
✔ Dental supplies (toothbrush, dentifrice)
✔ First aid kit
✔ X-pen, safety gate, or some type of enclosure
✔ Toys

activity level—also create some of the biggest problems for her safety and make her prone to accidents. Believe it or not, there are countless life-threatening situations in your cozy home.

A familiar toy or blanket will help your puppy travel better and feel more secure in its new home.

Be sure that you have removed any potential hazards before you let Annie explore and be sure that she is supervised at all times.

Household Cleaning Products and Chemicals

Cleaning products and chemicals are potentially deadly for Annie if she comes in contact with them. Some types of paints can be toxic if she chews on wooden baseboards or walls.

Be sure to keep the seat and lid down on the toilet. Many dogs will drink from the toilet and if you use any cleaning chemicals in the toilet tank, these can be very harmful.

Antifreeze

Antifreeze (ethylene glycol) is a major cause of animal poisoning. This common chemical can be found on garage floors. It has a sweet taste that attracts animals. Only a very small amount is required to cause severe kidney damage. Survival depends on an early diagnosis. If you suspect your car is leaking antifreeze, do not allow any pets in the garage.

Rodent Poisons and Snap Traps

If you have any rodent bait that has been left out for wild vermin, pick it up immediately. It is as deadly for Annie as it is for the wild rodents. If there are any dead rodents in the garage or yard that may have been poisoned, discard them. Scottish Terriers have an instinctive desire to investigate any rodent they find. If Annie consumes a poisoned animal, she can be poisoned as well.

Convenient Housing Options

Travel kennels	Ideal for use as small doghouses, lightweight, easy to clean, well-ventilated; provide privacy.
X-pens	Portable, folding pens, available in a variety of sizes; attachments for dishes.
Doghouses	Should be constructed of nonporous material; easy to clean and disinfect.
Safety gates	Useful for closing off a designated area or stairway to prevent escape or injury.
Bedding	Should be natural material (cotton, wool) because synthetic materials, or bedding containing cedar shavings, may cause allergies.

*Keep rodent bait and other poisons out of
your pet's reach.*

If you have snap traps set in your house or
garage, remove them. They can break small
toes or injure a nose.

Electrical Shock
Electrocution from gnawing on an electrical
cord is a real potential danger that could cost
Annie her life, and possibly cause an electrical
fire.

Kitchen and Appliances
It is not uncommon for pets to be burned
from hot liquids that have spilled from pots on
the stove, or from an iron falling on them from
the ironing board after a tangle in the electrical cord. Before you do the laundry, check the
dryer. Incredibly, some pets have been found,
too late, inside the dryer, where they had set-
tled in for a cozy snooze.

Doors
Make sure all doors to the outside or the
garage are closed. If Annie escapes outdoors
she can become lost and may become the victim of an automobile accident. To prevent a
broken tail or toes, be certain Annie is not in
the way when you close doors.

Injuries
Everyone in the house must pay close attention to where they step. Annie can dart out
from under the furniture and be underfoot
before you know it and can be stepped on and

*Make sure there are no poisonous plants in
your garden.*

injured. You also can be injured if you lose your
balance or trip and fall when you try to side-
step her.

Poisonous plants
Many ornamental plants are toxic to animals. Scottish Terriers have a natural desire to
dig and flowerpots and gardens are fair game.
Keep household plants out of reach and limit
home and garden plants to nontoxic varieties.

A bored Scottish Terrier can develop bad habits, like barking and fence pacing. Give your pet the attention it deserves and when you are absent, provide it with stimulating chew toys. To prevent escape from hole-digging, make sure the fencing extends several inches beneath the ground.

Foreign Objects

Dogs explore with their mouths and often will eat anything, even if it doesn't taste very good. If something is lying within reach or on the floor, you can bet that Annie will scout it out and sample it. Make sure small balls, children's toys, rubber bands, paper clips, pens, and anything else you can think of is out of her reach. Coins, especially pennies, are a particular hazard since they contain high levels of zinc and can cause zinc poisoning. Be sure that any toys you purchase are safe and do not contain small pieces, bells, or whistles that may be a choking hazard.

Garbage

It seems all dogs insist on exploring garbage cans. In addition to the obvious hazards associated with this activity, dogs may also suffer from "garbage poisoning," a form of poisoning caused by bacteria and bacterial toxins found in old and decaying foods.

Candies and Medicines

Make sure you have not left any foods or medicine containers within Annie's reach. An overdose of common medicines, including aspirin, acetaminophen (Tylenol), and ibuprofen (Advil), can be fatal for her. Chocolate contains a methylxanthine substance, similar to caffeine, called theobromine that is toxic to dogs. Hard candies can become lodged between the teeth at the back of the jaw or be a serious choking hazard.

Identification

The first thing you should do once you have brought your new companion home is to be sure she is properly identified. If Annie ever becomes lost, your chances of being reunited are very slim without proper identification. Ninety percent of all lost family pets are unidentifiable and 70 percent of these animals never return home. Annually 20 million lost American pets are euthanized. Don't let Annie become one of the statistics. If she doesn't yet have identification, stop whatever you are doing and have her identified right now. You'll be glad you did.

Microchips

One of the most recent, high-tech, and efficient forms of animal identification used today is by means of a microchip. A microchip is a microtransponder the size of a grain of rice that is implanted under the skin quickly and easily by injection. The microchip has a series of numbers unique to itself so that each animal has its own identification numbers. A hand-held scanner (also called a decoder or reader) is used to read the identification numbers. Microchips are safe, permanent, and tamper-proof. The entire identification procedure (microchip implant or scanning) takes only a few seconds. Scanning is absolutely painless and is accurate.

Once an animal has been implanted with a microchip, the following information is entered into a central computer registry:

✔ the animal's identification number;

✔ a description of the animal, the owner's name, address, and telephone number;

✔ and an alternate contact in case the owner cannot be reached.

It is the owner's responsibility to update the registry in the event of a change in information. An identification tag for the animal's collar is also usually provided, indicating the animal's identification number and the registry's telephone number.

Lost animals can be identified at animal shelters, humane societies, and veterinary offices. Once the animal's identification number is displayed, the central registry is contacted and the owner's information is released for contact.

Surprisingly, the cost for all of this technology, including the microchip and its implantation, is modest. In addition, the price for lifetime enrollment in the American Kennel Club Animal Recovery database is currently only $12.50. For the life of your pet, this is an investment you cannot afford to pass up on.

Collars and Nametags

Another excellent form of identification is a pet collar with your name and phone number clearly written on it. You can also have name tags engraved on the spot at many local pet stores. Collars and tags are easily visible and let others know your lost companion has a family.

Tattoos

Tattoos are a good form of identification because they are permanent. Your veterinarian can tattoo Annie at any age after weaning, usually with only a light sedation. Tattoos are usually done in the inner thigh, although the belly and inside of the ear are sometimes used. If you are having Annie neutered in the near future, ask your veterinarian to tattoo her at the same time while she is under anesthesia for the surgical procedure. There are tattoo registries where you can send updated information if you change address or telephone numbers. The American Kennel Club's Animal Recovery registers dogs that are tattooed or microchipped.

Housebreaking Your Scottish Terrier

Because Scottish Terriers are so smart, housebreaking is usually accomplished quickly. What's the secret? Patience, diligence, consistency, making sure your puppy gets to the right place at the right time, and lots of praise.

Scottish Terriers are meticulous about their living quarters and will do their best not to soil where they are housed or confined. This is another excellent reason for keeping Annie in a travel kennel on the way home from the seller's. If the trip was not too long, she probably will have waited to urinate or defecate. You can start out right by taking her outside immediately upon arrival and placing her right where you want her to learn to do her business. She will immediately urinate, and when she does, praise her repeatedly. You are off to a positive start.

The Proper Procedure

Next, place Annie in her designated living area. This area should have easy-to-clean flooring, such as tile or linoleum, but no carpeting. Remember that she has a very small bladder and does not have full control of bladder or bowels yet. She will need to go outside frequently and certainly will have a few accidents before she is fully trained. But remember that Annie wants to please. As soon as she understands that she should only urinate or defecate in the area you have indicated, she will try her best to wait until you take her to that spot. If she soils in her confinement, it is an accident, so don't punish her. The outdated and cruel training methods of rubbing a dog's nose in its urine, or hitting a dog, is the worst thing you could do. Don't raise your voice or reprimand Annie. She will not associate your scolding

TIP

Housebreaking Tips

1 Start house training Annie the day she arrives—it is never too early.
2 Let her outside several times a day— first thing in the morning, after every meal, after naps, and as late as possible in the evening.
3 Never scold Annie if she has an accident.
4 Praise her profusely when she does the right thing.
5 Be patient and understanding.

with her natural body functions, but she may become less sociable or withdraw from you. Everything is new and strange to her, and like a baby, she has little control over her elimination at this point. Rather, clean up the mess and work on positive reinforcement by praising her profusely when she does the right thing.

Annie doesn't know how to tell you when she needs to go, so for now it is up to you to be attentive to her needs and signs of impending urination or defecation so you can take her outside in time. Signs include sniffing the ground, pacing, circling, whining, crying, and acting anxious. You must act fast as soon as this behavior begins or you will be too late! Annie will always need to urinate immediately after waking up from a nap or eating a meal, so in these instances, take her directly outside without waiting for signs. Remember to lavish praise on her for her performance.

Ideally, a young puppy should be let outside every few hours. Of course, there will be times when you simply cannot be available to do this. When you have to be out of the house, or during the night, keep Annie restricted to her living area and place newspapers inside the confinement. She will do her best to urinate and defecate on the papers. Now she has the right idea and is learning to control her elimination until she reaches a given spot, even if it isn't yet the backyard.

Eventually Annie will be able to wait for longer periods of time as she develops more bowel and bladder control. It will be a while before she will be able to wait until morning to urinate, but during that time she will use the newspapers you leave on the floor.

Housetraining is the result of a two-way communication. You teach Annie that she must

Whether in the show ring or at the park, you will enjoy showing off your Scottish Terrier in tip-top condition. This champion's beautiful coat is the result of good care and nutrition, plus a lot of time, effort, and grooming skill!

eliminate outside and she must find a way to let you know her desire to go outside when nature calls. She may never "ask" to go outside by barking or scratching at the door or fetching her leash like the dogs in the movies. But if she hasn't been outside for a long period of time, or just woke up, or finished a meal, or starts to pant and stare at you, you know what to do.

Grooming Your Scottish Terrier

One of the joys of owning a Scottish Terrier is showing it off at its best. Regular grooming will keep Annie's coat and skin in top condition and is an important part of her health care program. Grooming should always be a positive experience for Annie and an enjoyable activity for you. Many Scottish Terrier owners groom their dogs as a form of relaxation and artistic expression. It is a documented fact that people can lower their blood pressure simply by touching or caressing an animal. Annie also will benefit from the close human contact and special attention received during the grooming session, and the massage sensation and skin stimulation a good brushing provides. The grooming session is a good time to check Annie thoroughly for signs of dry or oily skin, for lumps and bumps, parasites, stickers, and scabs.

Just as you will require some practice to become skilled at grooming, Annie will require some training to learn how to stand on the grooming table, what to expect of you, and how she should behave. A few minutes of training in the beginning is a necessary investment, otherwise, grooming sessions can turn into frustrating wrestling matches and a battle for dominance between the two of you.

Preparing for grooming is easy if you follow a few simple recommendations.

1. *Remember that several short training sessions are better than one long one.*

2. Begin training for grooming as soon as possible.

3. Designate an area to use exclusively for grooming. This should be an easy-to-clean, convenient location, close to an electrical outlet (for hair dryer, clippers, electric nail files, or vacuum cleaner).

4. Select a table that is high enough for you to work at a comfortable height, depending on whether you prefer to work sitting or standing.

5. Make sure the table has a nonslip surface to prevent falls or injury.

6. Invest in the best. Purchase quality tools and equipment, particularly brushes, combs, and scissors (blunt-tipped and thinning), and nail clippers. This will reduce your chances of developing blisters on your fingers, or sore wrists and arms from overexertion.

7. Place all the necessary grooming items near the grooming table, within easy reach.

8. Use only products designed for use on dogs to ensure a pH balance for canine skin, including emollient shampoos or spray-on dry shampoos.

9. Give a small food reward at the conclusion of each grooming session.

10. *Never leave any animal unattended on the table.*

The time and effort you invest in Annie's coat and skin will keep her looking in top condition. As you become more familiar with the Scottish Terrier standard, and develop more skill at grooming, you will find ways to groom Annie so that you can enhance her features to more closely reflect the ideal Scottish Terrier, while hiding any flaws.

Thinning the Coat

Most Scottish Terriers require some degree of coat thinning, depending on the thickness and texture of the coat, to eliminate dead hair and give a manicured outline. Clippers give quick results but tend to leave the dull, brittle hair in place along with the fresh, healthier hair. In addition, clipped coats tend to grow back softer, which is contrary to the American Kennel Club standard. Hand-stripping takes longer and requires skill, but the results can be more attractive and the desirable harsh coat texture is maintained. Hand-stripping is done by gripping a few hairs at a time rather loosely with the thumb and forefinger and pulling. The dead hair is plucked loose, and the healthy hair remains rooted. Hand-stripping should be done at least every 8 to 12 weeks to preserve the coarse texture. If done correctly, hand-stripping is painless.

If you make a mistake and remove too much hair, don't panic. The hair will grow back in time. However, some parts of Annie's coat will grow faster than others. Be careful not to remove too much hair from her hindquarters (the "drop" or "skirt") because it will take months to return. Always remember to comb the soft undercoat thoroughly to remove dander and keep the skin healthy.

Trimming the Coat

The coat should be trimmed to give an overall impression of a well-balanced animal with straight legs and a level topline. The front leg hairs (furnishings) should blend evenly into the shoulders. The back (topline) should appear strong and level.

Trimming the Face

A Scottish Terrier's head should not be trimmed excessively but it should not appear shaggy. The head should be trimmed to maintain the true Scottish Terrier expression. Comb the hair on the face forward just above the eyebrows and trim the head from above the eyebrows to the base of the skull, from the outer edge of the eyebrows to the base of the ear, and from the corners of the mouth to the throat. Oversized ears may require more hair removal to give the ears a smaller appearance. Trim some of the hairs from the inside of the ears so Annie looks neat and manicured, but not exaggerated. A pompon of hair should be left attached to the head in front of the inner edge of the ears. Whiskers on the sides of the face should be trimmed in such a way as to give the head a balanced look. The eyebrows

Cut only the curved tip of your pet's toenail, taking care not to cut into the quick where the blood supply is.

should be moderately trimmed (not too short!). A Scottish Terrier should never look harsh.

Trimming the Feet

Neat, trimmed feet look very tidy and prevent hairballs, dirt, foreign objects (such as grass awns), and excess moisture (leading to bacterial growth, moist dermatitis, and sores) from accumulating between the toes. Annie will walk better and track less dirt and debris into your home.

Trimming the Tail

Trim the tail to accentuate its short, strong, tapered appearance. Remove straggling hairs and blend the hairs at the base of the tail with the hairs on the body.

Toenails

Cutting toenails is something most dog owners dread, but it really isn't difficult. If you work with Annie's feet from the time she is very young, she will not mind having her feet handled and restrained. It is important to keep the nails trimmed so that they do not snag or tear, causing pain or discomfort. If the nails become too overgrown, they eventually will deform Annie's paws, interfere with her movement, and impede her ability to walk. In the most severe cases, overgrown toenails can curve under and pierce the footpads.

To determine if Annie requires a nail trim, stand her on the grooming table. None of the nails should touch the surface of the table. You will notice each toenail curves and tapers into a point. If the toenail is not too dark in color, you will be able to see pink inside of the toenail, or the "quick." This is the blood supply and just below it is the excess nail growth that you will remove. If Annie's toenails are too dark to differentiate where the quick ends, you can illuminate the nail with a penlight or a flashlight to find the line of demarcation where the blood supply ends.

There are different types of nail trimmers available. Most Scottish Terrier owners prefer the guillotine style clippers. To use these you

TIP

Trimming Toenails

If you accidentally cut a toenail too closely and you do not have styptic powder available, you may be able to stop the bleeding by pushing the end of the toenail into a piece of wax or a dry bar of soap. This will serve as a plug until the bleeding stops.

place the toenail inside the metal loop, aligning the upper and lower blades with the area you wish to cut, and squeeze the clipper handles. A good rule of thumb is to cut only the very tip of the toenail. If the nail is still too long, continue to remove the end of the nail carefully in small increments. If you accidentally cut too close, you can stop the bleeding by applying styptic powder (a yellow clotting powder commercially available from your pet store or veterinarian) or by applying pressure with a clean cloth to the toenail for five minutes.

When the blades become dull they should be replaced so they do not break, shred, or crack the nails. You may also opt to purchase an electric toenail filer to round off and smooth the nails after trimming. Be sure to praise Annie for her cooperation. Without it, nail trimming is virtually impossible!

Dental Care

Regular dental care and toothbrushing are very important aspects of Annie's health care program. Without good dental care and maintenance, plaque and tartar can form on the teeth. This formation makes the teeth look yellowish-brown and is caused by bacterial growth and food debris on the dental surface. Eventually the material hardens into a brown coating, starting at the gum line, and with time, covering the entire tooth. The gums also become red and sore from infection as periodontal disease develops. Periodontal disease causes more problems than swollen, painful, bleeding gums and tooth loss. The bacteria present in the mouth and gums can enter the bloodstream and grow on the heart valves or infect the kidneys and other organs of the body.

Brushing the Teeth

The best way to get Annie used to the idea of regular brushing is to start when she is a puppy. Her baby teeth will have fallen out by the time she is six months old, but they are good for practice and training. By the time her adult teeth are in, she will be used to the daily routine.

Purchase a soft-bristle toothbrush and dog toothpaste recommended by your veterinarian or local pet store. Do not use human toothpaste. Many human products contain spearmint or peppermint or other substances that cause dogs to salivate (drool) profusely or upset their stomachs. Use warm water. Cold water is unpleasant and may make the gums and tongue temporarily turn bluish in color.

Start with the upper front teeth (incisors) brushing down and away from the gum line and proceed back to the premolars and molars on one side of the mouth. You may also brush these teeth in a gentle, circular motion. Repeat on the upper teeth on the opposite side of the mouth. When you brush the bottom teeth, start with the incisors and work back to the molars, brushing up and away from the gum line. Repeat on the lower teeth on the opposite side of the mouth. Be patient. You may want to break the daily brushing into two sessions at the beginning. Spend about one minute on the upper teeth and then praise Annie for her good behavior. Later in the day you can spend another one-minute time increment on the bottom teeth, followed by profuse praise.

Good home dental care is a necessity, but it is not a replacement for veterinary dental visits. Even with the best of care, most dogs require routine professional dental cleaning and polishing.

Exercise

Exercise is an important part of all Scottish Terriers' physical and mental health. Scottish Terriers are by nature, busy, active, investigative dogs. They enjoy interesting outings and if left alone for long periods of time, they bore easily or get into mischief.

It is a general misconception that a Scottish Terrier requires a large backyard to keep in shape. What a Scottish Terrier really requires is a friend to develop a healthy exercise program suitable for her age, stage of development, health, and physical abilities. Annie can have the biggest backyard in the neighborhood, but if left alone all day, she will not exercise or work out on her own. She just might, however, dig up the flower garden!

When you begin to plan Annie's exercise program, remember that she first needs to build up endurance gradually. This requires a regular routine that, over time, may increase in length or vigor. Whatever you do, do not take Annie out for infrequent, strenuous exercise. Start with a moderate exercise program and build it up gradually to a level suitable for her age and health condition.

A regular exercise program will improve Annie's cardiovascular endurance and function, build strong bones and joints, and develop muscles and muscle tone. Before you start an exercise program, have her examined by your veterinarian and ask for exercise activity recommendations tailored to her needs and abilities.

Daily walks are among the best ways to exercise your Scottish Terrier (and yourself!) Play it safe. Always keep your pet on a leash during the walks.

Exercise Activities for Your Scottish Terrier

Walking or jogging: Walking or jogging is a great form of exercise. It is also strenuous, so start with short walks each day and gradually increase the distance or speed. Annie's natural pace is different from your own, so you may have to move faster or slow down to accommodate her so that she doesn't develop cramps or muscle spasms. Also, try to exercise on a soft surface, such as a lawn or the beach. Sidewalks and asphalt are hot, uncomfortable, and hard on the joints upon impact. Rocky or gravel surfaces are also hard on your pet's feet. Be sure to check Annie's feet for stickers, torn toenails, cuts, or abrasions at the end of every walk. Treat any sores and discontinue the walks until the lesions have completely healed. If you live in an area with snow, don't walk Annie on salted roadways and be sure to rinse her feet after each walk so she doesn't develop salt burns. Finally, try to work on level surfaces,

especially if she is young and still in her developmental growth phase, or if she is older, or suffering from arthritis. Climbing hills and stairs can be very hard on growing bones and joints, or aged hips and joints.

Swimming: Swimming is one of the best forms of exercise. It builds stamina and works most of the muscles in the body. Swimming is particularly good for older animals because it allows for exercise without impact or trauma to aged joints and bones. Never leave Annie unattended in the water. If she swims in a pool, be certain she knows where the stairs are and train her how to get out of the pool. Be sure also that she does not become chilled. Rinse out any salt water or chlorine from her hair and dry her thoroughly after each swim.

Fetch: Many Scottish Terriers will retrieve objects for their owners, although they are not always willing to immediately give them back! You can use a wide variety of interesting objects for this game, including balls, flying disks, and dumbbells.

Tracking: Scottish Terriers have a powerful sense of smell. If you want to make an interesting game for Annie, try hiding little tidbits around the yard for her to find. You can make the game more complicated by hiding the

treats one to two hours in advance of the search and increasing the distance between treats. The advantages to this type of exercise are that they encourage your pet to be active, increase her tracking ability, and you can set the course at your leisure. If Annie seems to have a natural ability for this game, you might consider contacting the American Kennel Club for a Tracking Regulations brochure. Annie might be a candidate for earning a Tracking Dog title!

Toys

Scottish Terriers love interesting toys, but they play rough with them! No matter what the purpose of the toy you purchase (for example, a ball to chase or a Frisbee to fetch), Annie will most certainly end up chewing on it. It seems all dog toys end up as chew toys, whether designed for that purpose or not. With this in mind, you should always be sure the toys you buy are durable and safe.

Chew Toys

Chew toys can enrich Annie's life by providing stimulation of the gums and exercise of the jaws, as well as helping to pass the time and avoid boredom when you are not home. Some chew toys help reduce tartar buildup on the teeth. Chew toys are useful tools to help keep Annie from chewing on valuables, such as furniture or clothing. Never give her an old shoe or piece of clothing as a chew toy. She will not know the difference between an old, discarded item and your most expensive clothing or shoes. By allowing Annie to chew on old shoes, you send the message that anything in your closet is fair game. Don't confuse her!

TIP

Toys

The best toys are those that cannot break or shred, are too big to be swallowed, and can also provide dental prophylaxis (gum stimulation and removal of tartar buildup on the teeth).

Dangerous Toys	Risks
Rawhide formed into bone shapes.	"Knots" of rawhide or other shapes can obstruct the trachea.
Latex toys, rubber toys, cotton ropes, hard plastic toys.	May shred or break and obstruct the gastrointestinal tract.
Toys small enough to be swallowed.	May obstruct trachea or gastrointestinal tract.

Not all toys are suitable for Scottish Terriers. For example, cow hooves, available as chew toys in local pet stores, are very hard and may actually cause a tooth to fracture. Other toys may break, shred, or tear and become lodged in the airway passages or gastrointestinal tract.

Travel Can Be Fun

Scottish Terriers love to travel and a well-mannered Scottish Terrier makes a wonderful ambassador for the breed. Whether you are on a long vacation, or a short outing, the company of a Scottish Terrier can make the trip all the more fun.

Travel Rules

There are a few basic guidelines you need to keep in mind to ensure the safety and enjoyment of your travels.

1. Make sure Annie is trained to her travel kennel and feels comfortable and secure inside of it. This training begins early in life, by using the travel crate daily as a security den and placing food tidbits in it periodically. When it comes time to take a trip, she will feel at home in her travel kennel and will not be stressed or fret.

2. Obtain a health certificate for travel.

✔ Make sure Annie is in excellent health and able to make the trip.

✔ Ask your veterinarian to conduct a physical examination and verify that all necessary vaccinations are up-to-date.

✔ Ask if any special medications for the trip are recommended (for example, medication for the prevention of heartworm in certain states, or medication for car sickness).

3. Make sure you have all the things you will need during the trip, including items in case of illness or emergency.

✔ Travel kennel

✔ Collar with identification tag and leash

✔ Dishes, food, and bottled water

✔ Medications

✔ First aid kit

✔ Toys and bedding from home

✔ Grooming supplies

✔ Clean-up equipment: pooper scooper, plastic bags, paper towels, and carpet cleaner

✔ Veterinary records and photo identification

4. Make reservations in advance.

✔ Check with hotels or campgrounds to be sure pets are permitted.

✔ Reserve space for a dog with the airlines if air travel is part of your travel plans.

Air travel: If you are traveling by air and Annie is accustomed to her travel kennel, tranquilizers are seldom necessary for air travel, are sometimes ineffective, and are often discouraged. Unless Annie is very young, and small enough to fit under the seat in front of you in a travel case, she will be assigned a space in the cargo hold. Be sure to make advance reservations, as there are a limited number of animals that may travel on a given flight, either in the cabin or in the cargo hold. The cargo hold is temperature controlled and pressurized just like the cabin in which you travel. Don't worry about your traveling companion—she will probably sleep better on the plane than you will!

Car travel: If your plans include travel by car, remember that some dogs have a tendency to become carsick. To reduce the likelihood that Annie will become carsick, limit her food and water three hours before travel begins and place her crate where she can see outside of the car. Although dogs become carsick from anxiety about travel, tranquilizers are not always effective in preventing carsickness. Another option you may wish to discuss with your veterinarian is the use of an antihistamine (Antivert, meclizine) that has been shown to be effective for some dogs.

Most important: Remember to never leave your Scottish Terrier in a parked car on a hot

day, even for a few minutes. The temperature inside of a car, with the windows cracked open and parked in the shade, can quickly soar past 120°F (50°C) within a few short minutes, and your pet can rapidly die of heatstroke.

Children and Scottish Terriers

The Scottish Terrier's appeal spans all ages. Children are drawn to the Scottish Terrier for its endearing appearance and small size. But children must be taught to respect these dignified, proud dogs and to resist the temptation to touch until the dog has had time to become acquainted. The Scottish Terrier is a stoic, tolerant dog, but it resents mishandling. It may be reserved and aloof around strangers. Be sure to teach children to approach Annie gently and to pet her only with permission and under your supervision. Scottish Terriers are not aggressive, nor are they quick to bite. However, they are loyal, devoted, and very protective of the family, especially children family members. Under the wrong circumstances, accidents can happen.

The first thing children should learn about any pet is not to put their face up close against the animal. It is very tempting to rub a cheek across the soft fur, or even try to kiss the animal, but this is the one thing they must not do. Because small children are short and their heads are large in proportion to their bodies, the majority of all animal bite wounds inflicted

Scottish Terriers are good swimmers. Your pet will enjoy a refreshing swim at the beach or the lake. Just be sure the area is safe for swimming and that your pet doesn't become chilled or overly tired.

A Scottish Terrier can make a wonderful companion for a child.

on children (regardless of animal species) happen in the area of the face and head.

Important Lessons

With adult guidance, there is no limit to the things children can learn from a Scottish Terrier. These wonderful dogs provide an excellent opportunity for adults to teach children about pets, the importance of humane care and treatment, and respect for life. They provide a way for very young children to learn responsibility by participating in the animal's care, learning the importance of fresh water, good food, a clean home, and a kind heart. Older children can learn a lot about animal behavior and biology, training, exhibiting, and respect for animal life. A Scottish Terrier is not only a dear friend to a child, it can serve as a confidant and a subordinate—something children rarely find. For a growing child, these are precious gifts that help develop confidence and character.

Some children are frightened or uncomfortable around dogs, especially large ones. Because a Scottish Terrier is small and appealing, it can make it possible for a child to replace anxiety, fear, or timidity with tenderness and affection. Adult supervision is necessary when a child is caressing a dog of any breed.

Even children who are somewhat shy often will talk freely when they are in the presence of animals. A Scottish Terrier can open doors of communication and learning for a child. While watching the animal at play, or taking it on a walk, a child becomes a captive audience and a good learner. Together you and a child can share thoughts and ideas about animals, people,

families, and anything else you can relate to Scottish Terriers and humans on the child's level.

Animal Life and Death

The most difficult thing about owning and loving a pet is the knowledge that even with the very best of care, old age or illness, and eventually death, cannot be avoided. Because Scottish Terriers have a relatively long life span compared to other kinds of pets, you and your family will have developed a long friendship and a deep attachment to this canine family member over the years. Children are very sensitive to issues of animal life and death, and the death of a family pet may be the first loss a child experiences.

It is important that the child is prepared in advance for the eventual, and inevitable, loss or death of a beloved pet. It is especially important that this preparation be provided in a compassionate manner appropriate for the child's age and level of maturity. The loss of a pet is an emotional experience for a child. But if handled skillfully, this loss can be turned into a positive learning experience.

In order to be an acceptable member of society, Scotty will need to learn some basic manners. Because Scottish Terriers are smart and eager to please, basic training is easy. Just remember that they are also independent and have a mind of their own. The trick is to make training sessions fun for both of you. Scotty will astound you with how quickly he learns his lessons.

A basic puppy class, or dog training class, is the most effective way to begin obedience training. There are as many different training techniques as there are dogs and trainers.

Dog training classes are a lot of fun. They are rewarding not only because your canine becomes a model citizen, but because you also will form many long, lasting friendships. Here are some training guidelines to get you started.

Come

Scotty must first learn his name so he can come when he is called and later respond to your commands. Start by calling his name when you feed him. It won't take him long to associate his name with a pleasant experience. In the beginning, you may also use small tidbits as a reward, along with much praise, when Scotty comes to you. Don't show him that you have a food reward. Keep him guessing. Over time, decrease the frequency of food rewards, but continue the praise. In no time at all, Scotty will come to you when called, purely for the attention you bestow on him, but that doesn't mean you still can't occasionally surprise him with a very small food reward!

Sit

Teach Scotty to sit by holding a small piece of food over his nose and raising your hand over his head. As his head goes up to follow the tidbit, his hindquarters will naturally go down and you may apply gentle pressure on the rump to help him sit in the beginning. Give Scotty a tidbit reward as soon as he is seated. As training progresses you may wait longer intervals before giving him the tidbit and eventually replace the food reward with praise.

Down

Teach Scotty to lie down by starting him in a sitting position. Kneel down alongside of him, on his right side, facing the same direction, and rest your hand lightly on his shoulders. Show Scotty a food reward and then slowly lower the food to the ground in front of him. This should encourage him to lie down to reach the food, but in the beginning you may have to apply light pressure to the top of his shoulders, or gently pull one leg out in front of him. Once Scotty is in the *down* position, praise him and give

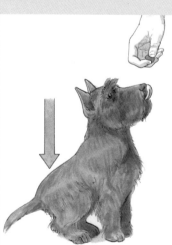

It is easy to teach your Scottish Terrier to sit. When your pet raises his nose to sniff the food reward, his hindquarters will naturally drop. Most Scottish Terriers can learn the "sit" command in a few short lessons.

him a food reward. As with other commands, you eventually will replace the food reward with praise alone.

Leash Training

After you have trained Scotty to come when called and to follow you around the yard, you are ready to begin leash training. Begin by attaching a light line, such as string or yarn, to his collar and allow him to drag the line behind him and to play with it. Encourage him to follow you with the string dangling along. When he has become accustomed to the string, replace it with the leash. Scotty quickly will adapt to the leash dragging on the ground and when he has, you can then pick it up and walk with him. Begin by holding the leash and following Scotty wherever he goes. This way he will not fight the leash or consider it a threat. He will probably ignore it.

As your training sessions progress, you will begin to guide your pet. Decide where you want to go, and with Scotty on the leash, encourage him with words and praise to follow you to that location. In the beginning the distance should be short, maybe just halfway across the backyard. If Scotty elects not to come along, simply stop where you are and wait. Don't drag him or pull on him. He may struggle against the leash at first, trying to get away, but he quickly will learn that any pulling or discomfort is created by his own activities and there is no resistance if he follows you. As soon as Scotty gives up the fight and approaches you or follows you, praise him for his common sense and end the training session shortly thereafter on a positive note with a food reward.

With patience, praise, and consistency in training, Scotty will be following along on the leash in no time. He may weave a bit, or run a little ahead, or drop behind for a moment to

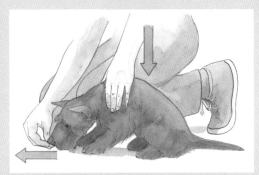

*The "down" command should not be attempted until the "sit" command is mastered. Some gentle pressure may be applied to the shoulders, but do not use excessive force. Once your pet is down, don't allow it to jump back up. A firm but gentle hand can hold it in the **down** position for a few moments. Remember to praise your Scottish Terrier!*

investigate something interesting on the ground, but he now will have the general idea. Once he reaches this level in his leash training, you can begin to work on fine-tuning him to heel.

TIP

Important Notes

✔ Keep training sessions brief and always end on a positive note.

✔ When Scotty requires a reprimand, use the word *no* consistently.

✔ Never use Scotty's name in connection with a reprimand.

✔ Always praise him for good performance and behavior.

✔ Train by using positive reinforcements (praise or food rewards) and not by negative reinforcement (scolding, physical punishment).

FEEDING YOUR SCOTTISH TERRIER

Good nutrition has been recognized for centuries as being one of the most important factors in maintaining health and extending longevity. Of all the countless things you do for your Scottish Terrier, providing a nutritionally complete and balanced diet is one of the most important ways to keep your dog healthy throughout life.

When dogs were first domesticated, their meals consisted of remains from the hunt, vegetables from the garden, and whatever "table scraps" were available. Dogs essentially ate much of the same foods as their owners. Due to the wide variety of foods in their meals, most of the nutritional bases were covered. Commercial dog food made its appearance thousands of years later, with consumer convenience in mind. As people became more pressed for time, particularly in the past forty years, we witnessed the evolution of TV dinners, microwave meals, and fast-food restaurants. The dog food business was not far behind, ready to capitalize on modern day lifestyles. It was obvious that families that spent less time cooking for themselves, were unlikely to cook for the family dog. Through advertising and excellent marketing strategies, the convenience of canned or pack-

Scottish Terriers are eager eaters. Your pet will be ready to join in on any picnic, but the food you eat is not always the best food for your pet!

aged commercial dog food was promoted until it became commonplace. Today the manufacture of pet food is a $15 billion industry. As with all businesses, success is measured by profit. This brings us to a key point to keep in mind as we review nutritional choices. Quality nutrition should not cost a fortune, but it is certainly not cheap.

The important role proper nutrition plays in a dog's life cannot be overemphasized. It is one aspect of health care in which you have full control and where you cannot afford to cut corners. It is the main key to overall health, development, and lifespan.

Starting Off Right

Before you bring Scotty home, ask the breeder what type of dog food he is currently eating and be sure to obtain at least a two-week supply of the food. Continue feeding the same diet, at least until he has had a chance to adjust to the new family and home. A change in diet during this time of adaptation can be stressful and can possibly cause stomach upset or diarrhea. Be sure to take Scotty to your veterinarian within 48 hours of purchase for a physical examination and to plan a complete health care program. The first veterinary visit is an ideal time to discuss specific nutritional requirements and the breeder's recommendations. If a change in diet is appropriate, make the change gradually by increasing the amount of the new diet and decreasing the amount of the old diet in small increments at each meal.

Changing Needs

Nutritional needs will change throughout life, so it makes sense that Scotty's diet also will need to be changed at times. For example, when he is just a puppy, he will need a dog food that provides complete and balanced nutrition for growth and development. As he reaches adolescence, his dietary requirements may lessen or increase, according to his individual needs and activities. When Scotty is an adult, he will have greater nutritional requirements if he is active, doing obedience work, on the show circuit, or being used for breeding purposes, than he would have if he were sedentary. Finally, as Scotty ages, or if he becomes sick or is recovering from an illness, he will need a diet based on his health condition and special needs.

Other Factors Affecting Diet

Environment also plays an important role in dietary requirements. If Scotty spends a lot of time outdoors in cold weather, he will have a higher caloric requirement to maintain his normal weight than if he stays indoors in a heated building most of the time.

Finally, genetics can influence a dog's caloric requirements, ability to digest and metabolize certain foods, and ability to maintain a normal weight. If some of Scotty's family members have difficulty maintaining an appropriate weight (if they are overweight or underweight), this may be an inherited tendency and you will have to make a special effort to closely monitor his food source and intake.

For each of Scotty's life stages, you should consult your veterinarian to learn which type of dog food would be most beneficial. The ideal nutrition for him today may not be suitable later in life. With increasing consumer awareness, dog food manufacturers certainly will make greater efforts to maintain a competitive edge and offer the dog owner a larger, more improved selection of dog foods from which to choose. For these reasons, nutrition always will be an important topic of discussion each time you visit your veterinarian.

Interpreting Dog Food Labels

Today there are countless brands and types of commercial dog foods from which to choose. Many claim to be the best food you could possibly offer your pet. But how can you be sure? Dog food comes in all sizes, colors, shapes, and consistencies (dry kibble, semi-moist, moist canned). You cannot help but notice how many brands are packaged and named to look and sound more like food for humans than for dogs. This is because the marketing is aimed at you, the consumer. But you are shopping for your dog and he doesn't care what color his food is. He does care how it tastes and smells. Even if you buy a very nutritious dog food, it will not benefit Scotty if he refuses to eat it. On the other hand, you don't want to feed an inferior formulation that is not nutritionally balanced simply because he likes the flavor. Sometimes the palatability and aroma that appeal to a dog are due to food additives, rather than nutrients (for example, artificial flavorings).

Anyone who has looked at dog food labels will agree that they can be confusing. A good way to select the best dog food is to consult with your veterinarian and Scottish Terrier breeders. Another way is to study the dog food labels and select a premium dog food that provides complete and balanced nutrition from high quality protein sources.

Here are some definitions to help you decipher and interpret dog food labels when selecting the best dog food formulation for your pet.

Ingredients

Ingredients are any of the materials used to manufacture a dog food mixture (proteins, fats, carbohydrates, vitamins, minerals) or non-nutritional (food additives, artificial colorings and flavorings, food preservatives). Ingredients are listed on the dog food label by decreasing order of preponderance by weight.

The list of ingredients provides general information about the types of ingredients found in the dog food, but it does not tell you about the quality, digestibility, or nutrient availability of the ingredients. Because different dog food manufacturers may use the same types of ingredients, but differ in the quality of the ingredients they use, do not rely solely on the comparison of ingredient labels on dog food packages to select dog food.

Nutrients

A nutrient is a substance eaten in order to maintain life. Some nutrients produce energy

(sugars, amino acids and fatty acids). Other nutrients do not produce energy (water, oxygen, vitamins, and minerals).

Nutrient Profile

The nutrient profile indicates the type and quantity of nutrients present in the dog food mixture.

Nutritional Adequacy

All dog foods (except treats and snacks) must contain a statement about the nutritional adequacy of the product (for example, "complete and balanced nutrition"). Current American Association of Feed Control Officials (AAFCO) regulations require nutritional adequacy be substantiated by either feeding trials or by meeting the AAFCO Nutrient Profile. Although feeding trials are the preferred method to demonstrate nutritional adequacy in a dog food, the more commonly used method is to calculate the formulation for the diet using a standard table of ingredients, without conducting laboratory analyses or feeding trials.

Proteins

Arguably the most important health factor in a dog's diet is protein quality. Dietary protein may come from plant or animal sources, however, not all proteins are created equally. In general, high quality animal source proteins provide a better amino acid balance for dogs than proteins from grains. There is a big difference between a high percentage of protein in the diet and high protein quality.

Some animal protein sources found in commercial dog foods include beef, chicken, lamb, fish, and eggs. However, just because the protein comes from an animal source does not

TIP

Food Dishes

Use stainless steel food dishes. Plastic or hard rubber dishes can cause skin allergies (contact dermatitis) in some animals.

necessarily indicate it is of high nutritional value. You must read the ingredients label closely and look for words such as "meat," "meal," and "by-products." Meat means muscle and skin, with or without bone. By-products include heads, feet, guts, and bone. By-products are usually a poorer and less expensive protein source. Meal indicates the protein source has been ground or reduced into particles.

Fats

Fats are important ingredients in the daily diet. Fats not only add to the flavor and palatability of the food, they are necessary for many aspects of an animal's health. They can play critical roles in clinical nutrition and therapeutic remedies, and influence skin and coat condition. Fats also aid in digestion, provide

energy, and are required for the assimilation of fat-soluble vitamins A, D, E, and K. The various fats (animal fat, vegetable oils, olive oil, fish oils) each have different effects on the body.

Carbohydrates

Carbohydrates are sugars, starches, and fibers. They are an inexpensive source of energy compared to high quality protein. These carbohydrates are usually provided in the form of corn, corn meal, rice, or a combination of grains. Because dogs cannot digest fiber, it is used in many dog foods, particularly weight reduction diets, to maintain dry matter bulk.

Note: Researchers have not yet determined the exact amount of carbohydrates required in the canine diet, yet carbohydrates make up the major portion of today's commercial dog foods.

Vitamins

Vitamins are necessary for good health and many of the biochemical reactions that take place in the body. Depending upon how vitamins are absorbed and excreted by the body, they are classified as fat-soluble (vitamins A, D, E, and K) or water-soluble (all the B vitamins and vitamin C). Dogs are capable of making their own vitamin C and do not require vitamin C supplementation in their diet (unlike humans, non-human primates, and guinea pigs, who will develop scurvy and die without dietary vitamin C).

Quality nutrition is essential for the health of your pet. Be sure to feed a diet appropriate for your pet's age, activity level, and health condition.

Vitamins must be correctly balanced in a dog's diet. Excess vitamin intake, or a vitamin deficiency, can cause serious medical problems.

Minerals

Minerals include calcium, phosphorus, sodium, potassium, magnesium, zinc, selenium, iron, manganese, copper, iodine, and other chemical elements. Minerals are necessary for skeletal growth and development, muscle and nerve function, and life sustaining bio-chemical reactions that take place in the body daily.

Like vitamins, minerals should be provided in a balanced ratio. Excessive supplementation of minerals can lead to serious medical conditions.

Additives and Preservatives

Additives and preservatives are substances added to the dog food to enhance color, flavor, and texture and extend product shelf life. Antioxidants are added to dog food to help

When you bring your puppy home, feed it the same diet it received at the seller's. If a dietary change is necessary, make it gradually, to avoid stress and gastro-intestinal problems.

keep fat in the food from becoming rancid over time. Other additives are used to delay bacterial and fungal growth.

Nutritional supplements are usually unnecessary if you are feeding your dog a high quality balanced diet.

Supplements

If you are feeding Scotty a high quality dog food, nutritional supplementation is most likely unnecessary. In fact, by supplementing him with other products, you may disrupt the nutritional balance you are striving to provide. Consult your veterinarian about any form of supplementation you are considering before adding it to Scotty's nutritional program.

Developing Good Eating Habits

✔ Designate a place for the dog food bowl and put everything Scotty is to eat in the bowl. This will discourage him from begging food from your hands or from the dinner table.

✔ Feed on a regular schedule.

✔ Do not feed Scotty human snack foods and candies. They are high in sugars and salts.

✔ Do not feed uncooked meat, fish, poultry, or eggs . These products can be contaminated with *Salmonella*, *E. coli*, or other bacterial pathogens that can cause fatal illness.

✔ Do not feed bones. They can splinter and become lodged in the throat or gastrointestinal tract.

✔ Determine in advance which food treats, and how many, Scotty will be allowed each day. Do not exceed the limit you have set.

✔ Feed snacks and treats primarily as training rewards or special praise.

✔ Teach children not to feed meals or give treats to Scotty without your permission.

✔ Do not allow Scotty in the kitchen while you are preparing food, or in the dining room during family mealtime. This prevents begging.

How Much to Feed

Nutritional needs will vary according to the stage of development, activity level, and environmental conditions. Basic feeding guidelines are provided on the dog food label, but the suggested amount per feeding may be more than Scotty requires. Just as you would not eat the same amount of food as your next-door neighbor, no two dogs are alike in their feeding requirements. Although there are all kinds of calculations you can do to determine Scotty's energy requirements and caloric intake, they will probably vary weekly, and possibly daily, especially if he is a young, active, growing puppy.

The amount you feed Scotty also will depend on the quality of the food you provide. If you feed a high quality dog food that is easily digested, a smaller amount will be needed than if you feed a mediocre diet filled with bulk and material that cannot be digested. You also will notice that Scotty will produce less fecal material when fed a quality diet, because most of the food is used for energy and less is going to waste.

The best way to know if Scotty is eating the proper amount is to check his overall physical condition. *You should be able to feel the ribs, but not see them.* Weigh him once a week, if possible, and not less than once a month. You can do this by holding Scotty and weighing both of you on a bathroom scale, then weighing yourself alone. Subtract your weight from the combined weight and the difference will be Scotty's weight. Another option is to ask your veterinarian if you can use the hospital walk-on platform scale each week. If you notice any weight loss or gain, your veterinarian can advise you if Scotty is within the appropriate weight range and whether to change the diet or meal size. Remember that an adult Scottish Terrier male should weigh between 19 and 22 pounds (8.6–10 kg) and a female should weigh between 18 and 21 pounds (8.2–9.5 kg).

When to Feed

Scottish Terrier puppies are active individuals that burn off calories quickly. Their initial growth phase is during the first 6 months of life, although technically they are still puppies until 8 to 12 months of age, or when they reach puberty. While Scotty is a puppy, he should be fed at least four times a day because he has a small stomach and a high metabolism. As a general guideline, when his growth and development begin to slow down, you can decrease the feeding schedule to three meals (at about 12 weeks of age), and later two meals (at about 6 months of age) a day. Be sure to consult your veterinarian to be certain this feeding schedule matches Scotty's specific needs.

Fixed Feeding Schedules

Unless Scotty is a hard-working, very active Scottish Terrier, he probably will not require more than one to two meals a day when he is an adult. Ideally the meals should be provided at 12 hour intervals, or if only one meal is provided, in the early evening, after he has exercised and before bedtime. If all of the food has not been eaten after twenty minutes, remove it. An after-dinner leisurely stroll before bedtime will help Scotty sleep more comfortably.

Free Choice Feeding

Some people prefer to feed free choice (also called "free feed" or *ad libitum*), which means that food is available at all times and the dog eats whenever it desires. This method works well for dogs that are nibblers, not gluttons. Although free choice feeding is convenient, it is difficult to know exactly how much food is eaten daily. It also is not usually successful because most dogs will eat even if they are not hungry. These gourmands eventually will exceed their ideal weight if food is not limited.

Obesity

Obesity is a form of malnutrition in which there is a ratio of too much fat to lean body tissue. We usually think of malnutrition as a deficiency in food rather than excess; however, malnutrition means improper (or bad) nutrition and refers to all aspects of unbalanced nutrition. Obesity in dogs has now

Weigh your Scottish Terrier once a week. An adult Scottish Terrier weighs between 18 and 22 pounds (8.2–10 kg). If you cannot feel your pet's ribs, it's time to go on a diet!

Above left: A beautiful coat and healthy skin are signs of good nutrition.

Above: No matter how mournful the regard, no matter how pleading the look, resist the temptation to overfeed your Scottish Terrier!

Left: Scottish Terriers are easy keepers and can put on excess weight quickly. Don't give in to their clever tricks to attract attention and tidbits!

Below: Don't let these puppy dog eyes trick you into overfeeding your Scotty.

Garlic and Brewer's yeast are ineffective treatments for internal and external parasites, but a little bit in the diet provides flavoring dogs enjoy.

With loving care and quality nutrition, your Scottish Terrier should live well into its teens.

You should be able to feel your pet's ribs, but not see them.

Bright eyes, a glossy coat, and excellent health are signs of good nutrition.

Scottish Terrier Growth Chart

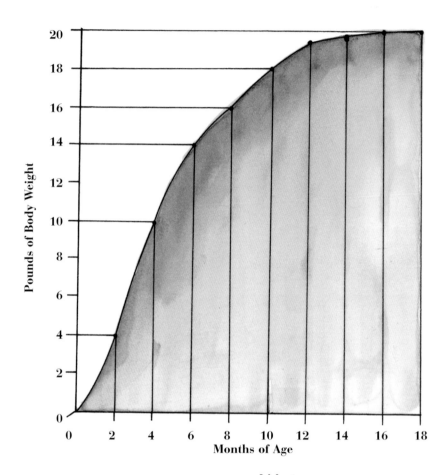

reached epidemic proportions in the United States—a staggering 30 percent of the canine population is obese. Overfeeding (especially overfeeding a puppy or adolescent) and inactivity can cause obesity, which in turn can lead to heart disease, skeletal and joint problems (such as arthritis), and metabolic diseases (such as diabetes).

Water

Water is the most important of all nutrients. Water is necessary for life because it is required for digestion, to metabolize energy, and to eliminate waste products from the body. Although you never would deprive Scotty of food, he could survive longer without food than without water. A 10 percent body water loss will result in death, and water makes up more than 70 percent of your companion's lean adult body weight.

Dogs lose body water throughout the day, in the urine and feces, by evaporation, panting, drooling, and footpad sweating. Water depletion occurs more rapidly in warm or hot weather or when an animal is active. Body water must be replaced continually so it is extremely important that fresh water be available at all times to avoid dehydration and illness.

It is important to monitor how much water Scotty drinks each day. If he seems to be continually thirsty or to drink more than usual, it could be a warning sign for possible illness, such as diabetes or kidney disease. If he is not drinking as much as he should, he can become dehydrated and develop a medical condition. Adequate water intake is especially important in older animals, as they may have impaired kidney function. If you think Scotty is drinking too much, or not drinking enough, contact your veterinarian right away.

Food Myths

There are some common food myths about the effects of various foods in the canine diet. Garlic is often credited with killing worms and repelling fleas. Brewer's yeast and onions also have been touted as flea repellants. Unfortunately, these foods have no action against internal or external parasites, although dogs can benefit from the B vitamins in Brewer's yeast. Onions, on the other hand, can cause toxicity in dogs and are not recommended in the diet.

Food Allergies

Just like people, dogs can develop allergies to certain foods. For example, some dogs are sensitive to corn (a major ingredient in many commercial dog foods) or corn oil, or beef in the diet.

Food allergies often express themselves by their effect on the animal's skin and coat. If Scotty is scratching his skin excessively, for no apparent reason, and his coat does not look its best, ask your veterinarian if a change to a hypoallergenic diet would be beneficial.

KEEPING YOUR SCOTTISH TERRIER HEALTHY

In earlier times, it was not unusual for dogs to die from a wide variety of health problems ranging from malnutrition, to severe parasitism, to deadly bacterial and viral diseases. The modern day dog is a lucky dog indeed, benefiting from all the medical advances, prescription products, good nutrition, and creature comforts that people enjoy.

Today's veterinarian has received years of training in medicine and surgery and many veterinary clinics are subject to inspection and accreditation. If Annie requires medical expertise in a specific area, board certified veterinary specialists are available to help.

It is reassuring to know so many resources are available if they are ever needed, but the best way to keep your pet healthy is to avoid or prevent problems before they start. Preventive health care is the most important care you can give your dog. It includes regular physical examinations, vaccinations against disease, an effective parasite control program, correct nutrition (see Feeding Your Scottish Terrier), regular exercise, good dental care, routine grooming (see At Home With Your Scottish Terrier), and plenty of love and attention to ensure Annie's physical and emotional well-being.

Your Scottish Terrier's health care begins the moment you bring it home.

Selecting a Veterinarian

You and your veterinarian will be partners sharing responsibility for ensuring your companion's health throughout her life. For this reason, you should be as particular about choosing Annie's veterinarian as you are about your own doctor. Fortunately, there is no shortage of excellent veterinarians, but how do you find the veterinarian that's just right for you and Annie? Here are some guidelines to help you in the selection process.

1. Ideally, you will want to find a veterinarian who appreciates Scottish Terriers as much as you do and who is familiar with the breed's special characteristics. Start looking for a veterinarian before you need one.

2. Ask satisfied Scottish Terrier owners and members of the local kennel clubs which veterinarians they recommend in your area. Word of mouth is one of the best ways to find a veterinarian. Many veterinarians advertise in telephone directories, but the size or style of an advertisement is not an indicator of the best match for your requirements.

3. Consider convenience. What are the doctors' office hours, schedule, and availability? Who is available on weekends and holidays, or in case of emergency? How close is the veterinary clinic or hospital? Will you be able to travel there within a reasonable amount of time in the event of an emergency?

4. Is there a consistency of personnel and continuity of communication? The veterinary support staff will play an important role in Annie's health care. Have the veterinary technicians (animal health care nurses) received formalized, certified training, and are they licensed?

5. What are the fees for services? Most veterinarians provide a price estimate for anticipated services and expect payment when service is rendered. Be sure to ask what types of payment methods are available.

6. Request an appointment to tour the veterinary hospital facilities. Examine all of the hospital during your tour, particularly as it concerns cleanliness and odors, the surgical suites and isolation wards, and the availability of monitoring equipment for surgery and anesthesia.

You and your veterinarian will develop a relationship of mutual respect and trust. You will rely on each other for accurate information and work together as a team. The chemistry among you, your veterinarian, and Annie should be just right.

Preventive Health Care

Physical Examinations

You know your companion better than anyone. You know when Annie is happy and feeling great, and you will be the first to notice if she is not acting herself, seems depressed, doesn't want to eat, is limping, is losing weight, or has any other problems. Of course, under these circumstances you would call your veterinarian to schedule an appointment for a physical examination, diagnosis, and treatment. However, the more you know about Annie's condition, and the sooner you recognize any potential problems, the more you can help her—and your veterinarian.

Home exams: A home physical examination is a good way to detect a possible problem before it becomes serious. The home examination is not a replacement for the veterinary examination, but gives you a good idea of your dog's health condition. If you notice something wrong with Annie, call your veterinarian right away and describe your observations and concerns. Keep a record of Annie's condition, noting the date and the time. Add information to the record if there are any changes. This information will be useful in assessing the progression or improvement of a condition over time.

In order to detect illness in an animal, you must first be able to recognize normal appearance, attitude, stance, movement, and behavior. Here are a few things to look for when you examine your Scottish Terrier.

1. First, watch Annie from a distance. Does she have a happy attitude? Is her coat glossy? Does she appear to be in good condition? Is she well proportioned (not too thin, not too heavy)? Does everything look normal or do you see anything unusual?

2. Observe Annie while she stands. Does she have a natural stance? Are her feet correctly placed? Does she place all of her weight on all four feet, or is she favoring one foot, or shifting weight from foot to foot? If she holds her neck outstretched, it may mean she is having difficulty breathing. If her back is hunched up she may have back or abdominal pain. What about her head and neck? Are they held in a natural position, or drooping? A dropped head may mean neck pain. Is her head tilted? This could indicate ear pain, ear infection, parasites in the ear, or a nervous system problem.

3. Make Annie sit and observe her position. Does she look relaxed and natural, or does she appear uncomfortable? If she holds her elbows out at her sides it may mean she has difficulty breathing.

4. Now watch Annie's movement and gaits. Does she walk, trot, and run willingly and normally? Or does she move with difficulty or limp? If she limps, does she limp in the front or the rear? Does she seem to experience pain, or wince when you handle her feet or legs? Does her head bob when she moves? If her head drops or dips more than usual, especially with every other step, it could indicate lameness. The origin of lameness is often difficult to detect, especially if the dog is lame in more than one limb. Lameness could be due to injury, joint problems, muscular or skeletal problems, or nervous system problems. Sometimes lameness is due to a foreign object, like a thorn in the footpad, or a grass awn lodged between the toes, so be sure to check all four of Annie's feet.

5. Now bring Annie in for the close up examination, from the nose to the toes. And yes, a cold, wet nose is normal for a dog, although a dry nose does not necessarily mean she is sick. The nose should be free of discharge (thick mucus or pus). With all her busy digging activities, Annie will get dirt lodged in the little "corner grooves" of her nose (the nares). This is

TIP

Temperature Taking

Normal body temperature for a Scottish Terrier ranges from 99.5 to 102.5°F (37.5–39°C). An excited dog may have an elevated temperature as high as 103.5°F (39.3°C), but it should not exceed this value. Use a digital thermometer to take Annie's temperature. Be sure she is sufficiently calm, so her temperature does not rise during the procedure. Lubricate the tip of the thermometer with petroleum jelly and gently insert it approximately 2 inches (5.2 cm) into the rectum. Wait for the beep signaling the temperature reading is complete.

normal and can be gently cleaned away with a soft Kleenex or cotton-tipped swab and warm water. If the nares become sore or raw, ask your veterinarian for some ointment to help protect it while it heals. You can also spread a thin layer of Vaseline or Aquaphor over the area, taking care not to plug the nasal passages. Frequent applications are usually necessary because dogs usually lick off medication on the nose shortly after it is applied.

6. Check Annie's eyes. Are they bright and clear? If the colored part of the eye(s) (the iris) appears hazy or cloudy, this could indicate a problem with the cornea, the lens, or the entire globe of the eye. Corneal injuries especially can be very painful and require immediate veterinary attention. Look at Annie's eyes in the light. The pupil (the black center) of each eye should match in size and shape. They should both

Your Scottish Terrier should sit comfortably and naturally. If it holds its elbows far out at its sides, this could mean it has difficulty breathing.

Your Scottish Terrier should have a normal stance; bright, clear eyes; a healthy coat; and an alert demeanor.

shrink in size in the sunlight and become larger when she is in a dark room. Check the eyelids. Do they fit properly over the eyes, or are they turned inward or outward? Do the eyelashes grow outward, or do they turn inward and rub on the surface of the eye? What about the white part of the eye (the sclera)? Is it clear, or is it red (bloodshot)? Check inside the bottom eyelids. They should be bright pink and free of discharge, debris, or pus. If they are pale in color, Annie could have a low red blood count and be anemic. If they are bright red, this could be a sign of inflammation. If there is pus inside the bottom eyelid, or in the corner of the eye, Annie may have an infection.

7. Look inside Annie's mouth. Do the teeth fit together properly? Are they free of tartar accumulation, or do they need to be cleaned and polished? Are the gums bright pink? Some dogs naturally have black pigment on their tongues and gums, but very pale pink, white, or muddy-gray colored gums, or a bluish tongue indicate serious illness in a Scottish Terrier. Does Annie have bad breath? It has been estimated that more than 85 percent of adult dogs suffer from some degree of periodontal disease and this can cause bad breath. Depending on the odor, some types of bad breath can also indicate a metabolic problem, such as ketosis.

8. Look inside Annie's ears. Does she shake her head or scratch at her ears? Her behavior could mean she has an ear infection or parasites, such as ear mites. It is normal for dogs to produce earwax, but excessive wax production, or very dark to black earwax, or a yellow discharge, require a professional examination and appropriate medical treatment.

9. Now look at Annie's hair and skin. Is the coat shiny? Is the skin healthy, or is it dry and

A Scottish Terrier is a bundle of power.
Movement should be effortless and animated.

Check your Scottish Terrier's eyes, nose, and
ears. They should be clean and free of discharge.

flaky, or greasy? Is there evidence of parasitism, such as fleas or ticks?

10. Moving on to the chest, you can observe Annie's body conformation as well as her ease in breathing and respiration rate. Can you see her ribs? They should not protrude but you should be able to feel them under a layer of muscle. If you cannot feel her ribs, she is too heavy. Although you may not be able to listen to Annie's heart well through her chest, you can take still measure her heart rate. To do this, simply press your fingers against the inside middle portion of her upper thigh. You will feel her pulse. Normal heart rate will range between 80 and 120 beats per minute, depending on whether she is at rest or has just been very active.

11. The abdomen should be tucked up neatly. It should not appear bloated or distended. Check the umbilical area ("belly button") and groin area for hernias. If you notice anything unusual, contact your veterinarian right away.

12. Finally, we come to Annie's "south end." If she has not been spayed, check her regularly for signs of estrus. You don't want to leave her within reach of unwanted suitors during her estrous cycle. If you have an intact male (not neutered), Scotty should have both testicles fully descended into the scrotum. If one or both testicles are missing, give your veterinarian a call. Retained testicles may be an inherited problem. If the retained testicle is not surgically removed, it can become cancerous in later life. It is wise to check Scotty's genital area periodically because it is not unusual for active dogs to accidentally bump and injure themselves. Finally, check under the tail for signs of problems such as swelling, hernias, anal gland problems, cysts, inflammation, diarrhea, and parasites (tapeworms).

Vaccinations

Vaccinations are the best method currently available to protect Annie against serious, life-threatening diseases. Although you will do your

Vaccination Schedule for Puppies

Vaccine	Age for 1st inoculation	Age for 2nd inoculation	Age for 3rd inoculation
Distemper	8 weeks	12 weeks	16 weeks
Hepatitis	8 weeks	12 weeks	16 weeks
Parvovirus	8 weeks	12 weeks	16 weeks*
Parainfluenza	8 weeks	12 weeks	16 weeks
Leptospirosis	12 weeks	16 weeks	
Bordetella	12 weeks	16 weeks	
Lyme Disease**	12 weeks	16 weeks	
Coronavirus***	8 weeks	12 weeks	
Rabies****	12 weeks	15 months	

*Some veterinarians recommend a 4th parvovirus vaccination at 20 weeks of age because some animals do not develop sufficient immunity against this disease before 5 months of age.
**Check with your veterinarian to see if Lyme Disease is a problem in your area or in any areas in which you will be traveling with your pet.
***Coronavirus vaccination may not be necessary. Consult your veterinarian.
****Rabies vaccination intervals vary according to state laws and the type of vaccines used. Consult your veterinarian.

best to prevent her from coming into contact with sick animals, at some time your companion will be exposed to disease organisms, whether you know it or not. Anywhere you take her—parks, rest stops, campgrounds, dog shows, obedience classes, or to your veterinarian's—Annie will be exposed to germs that could cause severe illness and possibly death. Although there is not a vaccine available for every known canine disease, we do have vaccines available for the most common and deadly diseases. No vaccine is 100 percent failproof, however, if you are conscientious about Annie's health and vaccination schedule, you can rest assured she has a very good chance of being protected against serious illness.

Vaccination schedules: You may note that veterinarians may recommend different vaccination schedules. This is because *vaccinations should be a medical decision, not a calendar event.* In other words, the type of vaccination and when it is administered should be appropriate to your Scottish Terrier's lifestyle, age, health condition, past medical history, and potential risk of exposure. Another reason vaccine schedules may vary is that most vaccine label recommendations are based on historical precedent. For example, it has been found that by vaccinating large populations of animals annually there has been a decline in disease incidence in the overall canine population. However, it has not yet been scientifically

Common Canine Diseases

Disease	Cause	Spread	Contagion	Symptoms	Treatment
Distemper	Viral	Airborne, body excretions.	Highly contagious, especially among young dogs.	Respiratory: difficulty breathing, coughing, discharge from nose and eyes. Gastrointestinal: vomiting, diarrhea, dehydration. Nervous: trembling, blindness, paralysis, seizures. Skin: pustules on skin, hard footpads.	None. Supportive therapy only.
Parvovirus	Viral	Contaminated feces.	Highly contagious, especially among puppies.	Gastrointestinal: diarrhea, dehydration,vomiting. Cardiac: heart problems and heart failure.	None. Supportive therapy only.
Infectious canine hepatitis	Viral	Body excretions, urine.	Highly contagious, especially among puppies and young dogs.	Liver: inflammation, jaundice. Eyes: "blue eye" due to inflammation and fluid build-up. Kidney: damage Pain and internal bleeding	None. Supportive therapy only.
Leptospirosis	Bacterial	Urine contaminated in kennels or from wild animals.	Highly contagious.	Kidney: damage and failure. Liver: damage and jaundice. Internal bleeding, anemia.	Antibiotics.
Parainfluenza Bordetellosis (Both cause "kennel cough")	Viral Bacterial	Airborne, sneeze and cough droplets.	Highly contagious, especially in boarding kennels and dog shows.	Respiratory: dry, hacking, continual cough of several weeks duration that may cause permanent damage to airways.	Supportive therapy, including antibiotics.
Coronavirus	Viral	Feces.	Highly contagious.	Gastrointestinal: vomiting, diarrhea, dehydration.	None. Supportive therapy only.
Lyme Disease	Bacterial	Spread by the bite of an infected tick or contaminated body fluids.		Swollen lymph nodes, lethargy, loss of appetite, joint swelling, lameness; can induce heart and kidney disease.	Supportive therapy, including antibiotics.
Rabies	Viral	Saliva (bite wounds).		Fatal, preceded by nervous system signs, including paralysis, incoordination, and change in behavior.	None. (Post-exposure treatment does exist for humans.)

Keep your puppy isolated from other dogs until it has had its second series of vaccinations.

demonstrated that vaccinations must be given every year. In fact, vaccines vary in range of purity, potency, safety, and efficacy. Vaccination is a potent medical procedure with profound impact. There are significant benefits, as well as some risks, associated with any vaccine. Vaccine administration should always take into consideration the animal's risk of exposure (population density), susceptibility or resistance to disease, and overall health (nutrition, parasites, age, special medical conditions).

For these reasons, the vaccination schedule on page 66 should be considered only as a guideline. Your veterinarian will determine Annie's vaccination program depending upon her needs and health at the time of examination.

Internal Parasites	Mode of Transmission to Dogs	Mode of Transmission to Humans	Prevention
Roundworms	Ingestion of eggs in feces of infected animals; transmitted from mother to pup in utero or in the milk.	Accidental ingestion of eggs from contact with infected fecal material.	Parasiticides should be administered to pups as early as 3 weeks of age and should be repeated regularly as necessary.
Hookworms	Ingestion of larvae in feces of infected animals; direct skin contact with larvae.	Direct skin contact with larvae in soil contaminated with feces of infected animals; accidental ingestion of larvae.	Parasiticides
Whipworms	Contact with feces.	No	Parasiticides
Tapeworms	Contact with fleas and feces; ingestion of fleas; eating raw meat (wild rodents).	Yes	Parasiticides
Heartworms	Mosquito bite.	No	Parasiticides
Protozoa	Contact with feces.	Yes	Parasiticides

You and your veterinarian will be partners in ensuring your Scottish Terrier receives the best medical care possible throughout its life.

Note: *Adult booster vaccinations should be given as recommended by your veterinarian based on your dog's health and specific requirements.*

Parasite Control

Giant strides have been made in recent years regarding parasite control, both internal (roundworms, hookworms, whipworms, tapeworms, and heartworms) and external (fleas, ticks, and mange-causing mites). Many products of the past have been replaced by recent, convenient parasiticides. For example, prevention and treatment of internal parasites, heartworm prevention, and treatment for flea infestation can be accomplished by giving your dog a single tablet monthly. There are a variety of pharmaceuticals available to prevent and treat internal and external parasites on a once-a-month basis. These effective, new products are available only from your veterinarian and require a physical examination, a heartworm test, and fecal examination, prior to dispensing.

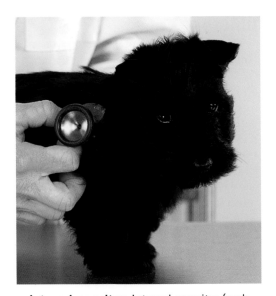

Internal parasites: Internal parasites (such as worms and protozoa) can have a serious impact on a dog's health. They can cause diarrhea and in severe cases, dehydration and malnutrition. In addition, many internal parasites of dogs are transmitted through contact with feces and can pose a serious health threat to people, especially children. This is why it is important to keep Annie in a clean environment and to teach children to wash their hands before eating or after handling any dog.

External Parasites	Animal Health Problem	Contagious to Humans
Fleas	Allergy to flea saliva; skin irritation and itching; transmission of tapeworms.	Yes
Ticks	Transmission of Lyme Disease; skin irritation and infection.	Yes
Sarcoptic mange	Skin lesions and itching, hair loss.	Yes
Demodectic mange	Skin lesions, localized or generalized hair loss.	No

Illness

If you have to ask yourself whether you should call your veterinarian, then it's a safe bet that you should. If Annie was looking and acting completely healthy and normal, you wouldn't be asking yourself that question. Better to be safe and contact your veterinarian if you think your pet is having a problem. Treating the condition at its very onset can make all the difference between rapid recovery and prolonged illness.

After conducting a physical examination on your companion, contact your veterinarian to discuss any abnormal or unusual findings.

Some abnormal findings may not be an illness in and of themselves (such as loss of appetite or listlessness), but they are good indicators that Annie is experiencing other medical problems that require veterinary attention. Contact your veterinarian if Annie is having any of the following problems:

✔ Fever
✔ Pain
✔ Loss of appetite
✔ Lethargy
✔ Vomiting
✔ Diarrhea

✔ Coughing
✔ Sneezing
✔ Wheezing
✔ Difficulty breathing
✔ Difficulty swallowing
✔ Choking
✔ Limping
✔ Head shaking
✔ Trembling
✔ Blood in the urine or stools
✔ Inability to urinate
✔ Inability to have a bowel movement
✔ Severe constipation
✔ Dehydration
✔ Weight loss

First Aid for Your Scottish Terrier

In spite of all your efforts to provide a safe environment for your Scottish Terrier, accidents can happen and many are life-threatening. The difference between life and death may depend on how prepared you are in an emergency situation. Be sure to have all your supplies on hand in advance so you do not waste precious time trying to find what you need to help her. As soon as possible, assemble a first aid emergency kit for Annie. Set aside a special place for the kit. Keep your veterinarian's daytime and emergency telephone numbers close by the phone and keep an additional copy of emergency telephone numbers in the first aid emergency kit.

If your Scottish Terrier has lost its appetite, is depressed, or shows any other signs of possible illness, contact your veterinarian immediately.

Supplies for Your First Aid Emergency Kit

There are some basic supplies and materials you will need for your first aid emergency kit. These items are available from your veterinarian or local drugstore. You will no doubt think of additional things to include in the kit for when you travel or are away from home. For example, bottled water, balanced electrolyte solution (Pedialyte), medication to prevent car sickness, tranquilizers, and pain killers (available from your veterinarian) are practical items to keep on hand.

First Aid Emergency Care

The goal of first aid treatment is to give Annie whatever emergency care she requires to save her life or reduce pain and suffering until you can contact your veterinarian. Before you begin any first aid treatment, the most important thing to remember is to protect yourself from being bitten or injured. An animal that is frightened, has been traumatized, or is in pain, will not behave normally and can be unpredictable. The friendliest of animals can and do bite when they are injured, in pain, or frightened. Your pet may not recognize you or may

First Aid Emergency Kit

Item	Purpose
Hydrogen peroxide 3 percent	Clean cuts and wounds, induce vomiting
Betadine solution	Clean and disinfect wounds
Neosporin ointment	Topical application to cuts and wounds
Kaopectate	Treat diarrhea
Milk of magnesia	Treat constipation
Ipecac syrup	Induce vomiting
Saline solution (sterile)	Flush and rinse wounds; can be used as an eyewash

Additional supplies:
1. Bandage scissors
2. Small, regular scissors
3. Thermometer
4. Tourniquet
5. Tweezers
6. Forceps
7. Mouth gag
8. Cotton balls
9. Q-tips
10. Roll of gauze bandage
11. Gauze pads (such as Telfa no-stick pads)
12. Elastic bandage (preferably waterproof)
13. Activated charcoal in case of poisoning
14. Muzzle
15. Blanket to provide warmth or to use as a stretcher
16. Paper towels
17. Exam gloves (vinyl is preferable to latex because some people are allergic to latex)
18. Flashlight

Check your Scottish Terrier's overall body condition. It should have a healthy coat and not appear bloated or overweight.

instinctively lash out in self-defense at anyone who approaches it. If someone else is available, you can save time by having the person contact your veterinarian for advice while you begin emergency treatment. You may need assistance restraining Annie while you treat her, so be sure the person assisting you is experienced in animal handling. *Always muzzle your dog before initiating emergency treatment, for the safety of your pet and everyone involved.*

Bite wounds: Scottish Terriers generally will not initiate a fight, but when a fight breaks out, they won't back down. Bite wounds commonly result from battles with other dogs, cats, or wild animals. In addition to thorough cleansing, bite wounds usually require antibiotic therapy to prevent infection. If the wound is a tear, it may need to be sutured. If the injury is a puncture wound, it should be cleaned well with hydrogen peroxide and allowed to remain open and drain.

Be sure to consult your veterinarian immediately regarding any bite wound injuries. Antibiotics may be necessary to prevent bacterial infection. In addition, if a stray animal or a wild animal (raccoon, skunk, bat) has bitten Annie, you need to discuss the possible risk of rabies in your area with your veterinarian.

Bleeding: Bleeding can occur from injury, trauma, or serious health problems. The first thing you should do is to apply firm pressure over the wound to stop the bleeding. If you do not have a gauze or clean towel, any readily available, clean, absorbent material can be used as a compress. If a large blood vessel in a limb has been severed, it may be necessary to apply a tourniquet above the cut area. A small percentage of Scottish Terriers have blood disorders that cause their blood to clot slower than usual, or to not clot at all. (See Selected Diseases and Conditions in Scottish Terriers.) If blood loss is severe, your pet can go into shock and die. Contact your veterinarian immediately.

Bloat: Bloat (gastric dilatation) is distension of the stomach, caused by the accumulation of trapped gas. It is a very painful condition that is life threatening. Bloat usually occurs after excessive activity following consumption of a large meal. As gases build up, the stomach or intestines can twist and the circulation can be blocked. As the animal becomes more bloated, it has difficulty breathing and the pain becomes more intense. Symptoms of bloat include a distended abdomen, retching motions, panting, restlessness, drooling, sitting with elbows pointed away from the body, and eventually collapse, coma, and death.

Bloat is more common in large, deep-chested breeds, but can occur in other breeds. It is a serious emergency situation that requires immediate, urgent treatment to save the animal from a painful death. If you suspect Annie is suffering from bloat, contact your veterinarian immediately.

Bone fractures: Signs of bone fractures include swelling, pain and tenderness, abnormal limb position or movement, limping, and crepitation (crackling sensation when the area is touched). When bones are broken, they may remain under the skin or protrude up through the skin (open fracture).

If Annie breaks a leg, and the bone is not exposed, you can make a temporary splint out of a piece of wood or folded newspaper or magazine. First, muzzle your Scottish Terrier. Then gently tape the splint to the leg, allowing a six-inch overlap at each end of the break site. Do not wrap the splint to the leg so tightly that the paw swells and do not wrap tape on the injury. If the bone is exposed, do not try to replace it or cleanse it. Stop the bleeding and cover the wound with a sterile bandage. Make sure Annie does not contaminate the open fracture by licking it. Contact your veterinarian immediately for advice. Annie should receive veterinary care for the broken bone(s) as soon as possible, and definitely within 24 hours.

Burns: Your Scottish Terrier can suffer three kinds of burns:
✔ Thermal burns—fire, boiling liquids, appliances
✔ Electrical burns—usually caused from chewing on electrical cords
✔ Chemical burns—from a variety of chemicals (such as corrosives, oxidizing agents, desiccants, and poisons)

If Annie is burned, immediately cool the burn by applying a cold, wet cloth or an ice pack to the area. Protect the burned area from the air with an ointment (Neosporin or *Aloe vera*). If she has suffered a chemical burn, immediately flush the burn profusely with water or saline to dilute and rinse the caustic chemical from the area. Do not allow Annie to lick the area or she will burn her mouth and esophagus with the substance. Contact your veterinarian immediately.

Choking: Choking occurs when an object (bones, food, toys, rocks) becomes trapped, or lodged, in the mouth or throat. In this case, your pet is in immediate danger of accidentally inhaling the foreign object. If the object obstructs the air passageway, Annie will suffocate. If she is choking, you will need a good, clear view of her mouth and throat to see if the offending object can be found and safely

If your pet is not feeling well, place it in a quiet area where it can rest and contact your veterinarian. The sooner you identify and treat your companion's problem, the better its chances for a speedy recovery.

removed. Scottish Terriers have powerful jaws. It will be difficult to pull Annie's jaws open to look into her mouth. Watch your fingers and be careful not to get bitten. A short wooden dowel, 2 to 3 inches (5–6 cm) in diameter, inserted between the back molars, may serve as a gag to hold the mouth open while you use a flashlight to take a closer look down the throat. If you see the foreign object, be very careful not to push it further down the throat or into the trachea (windpipe). Remove the object with forceps when possible, to avoid being bitten.

Cuts: Cuts should be cleansed well and treated properly to prevent infection. Sometimes it is difficult to tell how deep the cut is. Serious cuts may require sutures, so be sure to contact your veterinarian for advice. If the cut is not too deep, wash it with a mild soap and rinse it several times with water. Disinfect the injury with hydrogen peroxide or Betadine solution (hydrogen peroxide is especially useful for treating puncture wounds). Dry the wound well and apply an antibiotic ointment to it. If the cut is in an area that can be bandaged, wrap the area with gauze and elastic bandage to prevent contamination and infection. Change the bandage daily.

Dystocia: Dystocia is the term used when a pregnant female has difficulty giving birth to her young. Dystocia occurs when the smooth muscles of the uterus become fatigued and weakened and can no longer contract. Dystocia also occurs when the uterus becomes twisted, or when the mother's pelvic area is abnormal or too small to allow passage of the fetus. In some cases, dystocia occurs because the fetus is too large or not in an appropriate birth position. (It is normal for puppies to be born either hindfeet and rump first, or head first.)

Dystocia is not unusual among Scottish Terriers. It is a medical emergency that requires veterinary expertise. Medications to stimulate uterine contractions, or surgery, may be required to successfully deliver live pups. For this reason it is a good idea to give your veterinarian advance notice of Annie's delivery due date and make back-up arrangements for emergency care if your veterinarian is unavailable the day she gives birth (whelps).

A good rule of thumb is to not allow Annie to be in hard labor for more than two hours. If she has not whelped a pup within that time period, or if she has stopped labor altogether, she needs help. Contact your veterinarian immediately.

Heatstroke: Heatstroke is caused by exposure to high temperature and stress. Confinement in a car is one of the leading causes of heatstroke. On a hot day, a car parked in the shade, with the windows partially open, can still reach temperatures exceeding 120°F (48.4°C) within a few minutes. Overexertion on a hot day can also cause heatstroke. Dogs that are old or overweight are especially prone to heatstroke.

Signs of heatstroke include rapid breathing, panting, bright red gums, vomiting, diarrhea, dehydration, and a rectal temperature of 105 to 110°F (41–43°C). As the condition progresses, the body organs become affected, the animal weakens, goes into shock, then a coma, and dies. All of this can happen in a very short period of time and death can occur rapidly.

If Annie is suffering from heatstroke, you must lower her body temperature immediately. You can do this by placing her in a tub filled with cold water. Be sure to keep Annie's head above the water, especially if she is unconscious, so that she does not drown. Do not try to give Annie water to drink if she is unconscious. If a tub is unavailable, you can cool your pet by hosing her with a garden hose or applying ice packs to her body.

Heatstroke is a medical emergency that requires veterinary care. Annie will need to be treated with intravenous fluids and various medications to treat shock and prevent cerebral edema (brain swelling). Contact your veterinarian immediately.

Eye injury: Eye injuries are extremely painful. The sooner you obtain treatment for Annie's eyes, the sooner you can relieve your companion's pain and increase the chances of saving her eyes and vision. Injured eyes are very sensitive to the light and exposure to even subdued lighting can hurt the eyes. If Annie's injury is such that it requires flushing and rinsing the eye, you can do this using a commercial eyewash solution or saline solution intended for use in the eyes. Place Annie in a dark place and contact your veterinarian immediately. When you transport her to the hospital, place her in a travel crate and cover the crate with a blanket to keep out as much light as possible.

Insect stings: If a bee stings Annie, remove the stinger with tweezers. (Wasps and hornets do not leave their stingers.) Try to gently remove the stinger without squeezing the base (where part of the bee's body is attached) so that additional venom is not injected into the site. This can be tricky, as the bee's stinger is barbed and the more you push on it, the deeper it penetrates.

Apply baking soda or an ice pack to the area to relieve pain. You may also put a topical antihistamine cream around the stung area.

Watch Annie closely for the next two hours for signs of illness.

Most cases of bee, hornet, and wasp stings are painful annoyances. However, some animals develop a hypersensitivity to insect stings that can lead to anaphylactic shock and death. If the swelling worsens, or if Annie becomes restless and has difficulty breathing, or starts to vomit, develops diarrhea, or loses consciousness, contact your veterinarian immediately. This is a life-threatening situation and immediate professional treatment is necessary.

Poisoning: In addition to insect venom poisons, pets can be poisoned by eating or inhaling toxic substances, or by contact with poisons on their skin, mucus membranes, or eyes.

Signs of poisoning include restlessness, drooling, abdominal pain, vomiting, diarrhea, unconsciousness, seizures, shock, and death. Common sources of poison include rodent bait, houseplants, insecticides, medication overdose, spoiled food, antifreeze (ethylene glycol), and chocolate. (Chocolate contains theobromine, a substance similar to caffeine, that is toxic to dogs.)

If you know the source of Annie's poisoning, contact your veterinarian immediately for advice. If the poison came in a container (for example, antifreeze or rodent poison), read the container label and follow the emergency instructions for treating poisoning. If the instructions state to induce vomiting, you may accomplish this by administering ½ ml of syrup of ipecac per pound of body weight or ½ teaspoon of hydrogen peroxide, 3 percent for every ten pounds of body weight.

Activated charcoal is a good compound to use to dilute and adsorb ingested poisons. You can obtain activated charcoal in powder or tablet form from your veterinarian to keep in

Protect your pup by having a first aid kit prepared for any emergency.

TIP

Muzzles

If you have not yet purchased a muzzle from the pet store, you can make a muzzle using rolled gauze or a cloth strip about two and one-half inches wide and 30 inches long.

Wrap the gauze over the muzzle, making sure it does not pull on all the hair around the face, and tie it securely under the chin (this will not affect Annie's ability to breath). Take the ends of the gauze and tie them behind the head, on top of the neck. This muzzle will not hurt your pet and will protect you from being bitten. Make sure your Annie does not try to remove the muzzle with her front paws.

your first aid kit. If you do not have activated charcoal, and you do not have any products to induce vomiting, you can dilute the poison in the gastrointestinal tract by giving Annie some milk. Do not try to give her any medication if she is unconscious.

The sooner the poisoning is diagnosed and treated, the better Annie's chances of full recovery. Most poisonings require veterinary treatment in addition to the initial emergency care you provide. Contact your veterinarian immediately if you suspect Annie has been exposed to poison.

Porcupine quills: Scottish Terriers are determined, tenacious hunters. If you live in the country, at some time your companion will likely encounter a porcupine. These large rodents sport some very impressive, barbed quills that serve as an excellent form of defense. Sharp barbs enable the quills to migrate deep into the tissues, causing pain and infection until they are so deeply embedded the quills can be difficult to find.

If Annie has had an encounter with a porcupine, check first to make sure her eyes have not been injured. If a quill has penetrated her eye(s), call your veterinarian immediately. Almost all porcupine quills are found in the face, mouth, tongue, cheeks, chest, and front legs.

Muzzle Annie and remove the quills as soon as possible so they do not migrate deep into the body tissues. Gently remove the quills with a pair of pliers or forceps. Pull straight out so that you do not bend or break the quills. Disinfect the external areas with hydrogen peroxide or Betadine solution. Check the inside of the mouth, cheeks, tongue, and gums thoroughly for quills. Contact your veterinarian.

Skunk spray: At some time or another during an outing, Annie may discover a skunk.

Skunks are small, reclusive, shy, nocturnal animals closely related to minks, ferrets, badgers, and otters. Skunks have two methods of self-defense: warning coloration in the form of an unusual black coat with broad white strips or white spots, making them easy to recognize and avoid, and anal glands that can accurately spray a potent, bright yellow musk with an offensive odor. In the face of danger, a skunk will try to escape, but if cornered or harassed it will threaten with handstands and foot stomping and end the performance by spraying its attacker. Skunk spray stings the skin and eyes and has been reported in some cases to cause brief, transient blindness. These effects are temporary and Annie will be all right. If she has been sprayed in the eyes, rinse the eyes profusely with a mild eyewash. Several minutes of soft spray from a water hose, followed by some soothing ophthalmic solution is also a good way to rinse skunk spray from the eyes. You can purchase a shampoo specially formulated to neutralize skunk odor (such as Skunk-Off) from your veterinarian or local pet store. Most Scottish Terriers learn their lesson after the first skunk encounter, recognizing the skunk's warning coloration. Other Scottish Terriers never give up the hunt and are repeatedly sprayed.

Seizures: There are many causes of seizures, including epilepsy, poisoning, and brain trauma. Seizures may be mild or severe, ranging from a mild tremor of short duration, to violent convulsions, chomping jaws and frothing at the mouth, stiffening of the neck and limbs, and cessation of breathing. During a severe seizure, a dog is not conscious and can be hurt thrashing about on the floor. Annie may seem to be choking during a seizure, but avoid the temptation to handle her mouth as you will be bit-

TIP

Home Recipe for Eliminating Skunk Odor on Dogs

Mix together
✔ 1 quart 3 percent hydrogen peroxide
✔ ¼ cup baking soda
✔ 1 teaspoon liquid soap
　Bathe dog with solution. Do not allow the mixture to come into contact with your pet's eyes. Rinse thoroughly with tap water.
　The soap acts to break up the oils in the skunk spray, allowing the other ingredients to neutralize the thiols that cause the odor.

ten. If her jaws clamp down on your fingers, the jaws will not release until the seizure has ended. Simply try to prevent Annie from injuring herself or hitting her head until the seizure has ended. After a seizure, Annie will be exhausted and seem dazed. Place her in a quiet room with subdued light. Keep her comfortable and warm and when she is conscious offer her some water to drink. Contact your veterinarian immediately for follow up medical care and to determine the cause of the seizure and how to prevent another one from occurring.

Shock: Shock is a condition in which there is a decreased blood supply to vital organs and the body tissues die from inadequate energy production. Blood loss, heatstroke, bacterial toxins, and severe allergic reactions can all cause an animal to go into shock.

Shock is a serious emergency situation that results in a rapid death unless immediate veterinary care, including fluid and oxygen therapy and a variety of medications, is available. Signs of shock include vomiting, diarrhea, weakness, difficulty breathing, increased heart rate, collapse, and coma.

Snakes, toads, lizards, and spiders: Because your Scottish Terrier is an adventurer who doesn't miss a thing, it is important to be aware of additional risks she may encounter away from home, particularly on camping trips.

Poisonous snakebites. There are three groups of venomous snakes in North America: the pit vipers, which include the rattlesnake, copperhead, and water mocassin (also known as the cotton mouth); the coral snakes; and the colubrids. The pit vipers and coral snakes are the most important. Rattlesnake bites occur most frequently in dogs, particularly in the west and southwest where rattlesnakes are common. The snake's bite produces painful, slit-like, puncture wounds that rapidly become swollen. Common symptoms of snakebite include immediate severe pain, swelling, darkened tissue coloration, and tissue necrosis (tissue death).

Urgent, immediate, veterinary attention is necessary. The lethality of the snakebite depends upon the type of venom and its toxicity, the amount of venom injected, the size and health of the bitten victim, and the amount of time that passes from the time of the bite until medical care is provided. Poisonous snakebites require antivenin and antibiotic treatments. If the bite is left untreated, the skin and underlying tissue may turn dark and slough off (rot). However, the amount of venom injected (envenomation) cannot be determined simply by the appearance of the bite wound. The bite victim may become weak and exhibit various neurological signs, such as respiratory depression, and eventually go into shock and die.

If a venomous snake bites Annie, contact your veterinarian immediately. Most veterinarians who practice in areas where snakebites are common keep antivenin available. All dogs bitten by venomous snakes should be hospitalized and monitored for at least 24 hours.

Toad poisoning. Poisonous toads in the United States include the Colorado Rim Toad and the Marine Toad. The most toxic toad varieties are located in the southwestern desert and southeastern United States and Hawaii. If you suspect Annie has come in contact with a poisonous toad, contact a veterinarian immediately for specific treatment recommendations.

Lizard bites. The poisonous Gila Monster lizard is found in the southwestern United States. It has grooved teeth (instead of fangs) with which it holds onto its victims. Most dogs are bitten on the upper lip. The Gila Monster bite is extremely painful. No antivenin is available. Contact your veterinarian immediately for supportive treatment, antibiotics, and treatment to prevent shock.

Spiders. The brown spiders (Fiddleback, Brown Recluse, and Arizona Brown Spider) are all found in the southern United States. There is no antidote available for their venomous bites. Black widow spiders are found throughout the United States. There is an antivenin available for Black Widow bites.

If Annie is bitten by one of these spiders, take her to a veterinarian immediately for emergency care, antibiotic therapy, and antivenin therapy (for Black Widow spider bite).

The Senior Scottish Terrier

With tender loving care, good nutrition, and a little luck, your Scottish Terrier may live for

12 years or more. Just like people, some dogs age more slowly than others, especially those that have received good health care throughout their lives. As a general rule, a Scottish Terrier is not quite a senior citizen until it reaches seven years of age. Scottish Terriers are stoic and keenly alert, so it may not be easy to see some of the first signs of age, such as joint pain, poor vision, hearing loss, and a greater reliance upon sense of smell. As Annie's body ages, it undergoes a slowing of metabolic rate that can lead to weight gain; a weaker heart and a reduction in kidney and liver function; tooth loss and periodontal disease; cataracts; joint degeneration; skin and hair problems; general muscle weakening and atrophy; and a gradual deterioration in condition with a decreased resistance to diseases. Annie may even show signs of disorientation or senility. All of these age-related changes, and the rate at which they occur, vary between individuals and are influenced by genetics, nutrition, environment, and the type of health care received in earlier years.

Golden Years Care

There are a number of things you can do to keep Annie comfortable in her golden years.

1. Provide a soft, warm bed. Cold temperatures and hard surfaces make arthritis more painful.

2. Weigh Annie monthly and do not allow her to become over- or underweight.

3. Take Annie out regularly for easy, short, walks on level, soft, nonslippery, surfaces (such as grass). Keep her toenails trimmed.

4. Do not make Annie climb stairs or hills, jump in and out of cars, or walk on slippery surfaces.

5. Feed Annie a diet appropriate for her age and health condition. Old dogs have an increased protein requirement. An increase in protein quality and quantity recently has been demonstrated to be beneficial for some geriatric dogs, as well as having anticancer and antidiabetes effects.

6. Schedule physical examinations for Annie every six months in her geriatric years. This way, you can detect and address any age-related problems (such as cataracts, heart or kidney insufficiency) early. Remember that older dogs are more sensitive to anesthesia, especially if they are overweight.

7. If Annie has failing eyesight or is hard of hearing, make every effort not to startle her. Speak to her reassuringly as you approach so she knows you are there.

Euthanasia—When It's Time to Say Good-bye

Euthanasia means putting an animal to death humanely, peacefully, and painlessly. There are different ways veterinarians euthanize animals, depending on the circumstances. Euthanasia is usually done by first giving the animal a sedative to make it sleep deeply and then giving it a lethal substance by injection that ends its life almost instantly.

Even with the best care in the world, the sad day will come when you must consider euthanasia for your beloved companion. This, understandably will be an emotionally painful time for you because you will feel helpless in your inability to help your friend any more. You will not want her to suffer for a moment, yet you will not be able to bear the thought of life without her. Nevertheless, if you begin to

With good care and nutrition, your Scottish Terrier will live well into his golden years.

ask yourself whether your pet should be euthanized, there must be good reasons. The decision of when to euthanize is a difficult one that depends upon many things. A good rule of thumb is, if suffering cannot be relieved, or if the quality of life is poor, or if the "bad days" simply outnumber the "good days," it is time to discuss euthanasia with your veterinarian. Your veterinarian can answer any specific questions

you or your family may have. Your veterinarian can also help you if you wish to find a pet cemetery or desire cremation services.

During this emotional time, remember to take care of yourself and allow time to grieve. If you have children in the family, deal with the issue of animal loss at a level they can understand, comfort them, and let them share their grief. (See Children and Scottish Terriers.) Take comfort in the knowledge that you took excellent care of your Scottish Terrier throughout her life and that you made the best decisions regarding her health and welfare, even when you had to make the most difficult decision of all.

Selected Diseases and Conditions in Scottish Terriers

Scottish Terriers are hardy, sturdy, resilient dogs. Throughout the century they have been recognized for their stamina and their ability to survive harsh conditions. But like every other breed of dog, or animal species, Scottish Terriers can have problems. Each breed of dog is predisposed to various conditions or disorders. This does not mean that the problems are unique to a specific breed. Many dog breeds share the same health problems. It also doesn't mean your dog will ever experience any of these problems, or that the problem is widespread within the breed. It simply means that when there are problems, these are the types most commonly observed in the breed. So don't let this list frighten you. Most likely, Annie will not have any of these conditions, but if she does, this list will help you recognize the problem at the onset.

Condition	Type of problems	Heritability*
Blood disorders: 1. Autoimmune hemolytic anemia 2. Hemophilia B 3. Thrombasthenic thrombapathia 4. von Willebrand's disease	Characterized by anemia, destruction of red blood cells, defects in blood plasma, and platelet aggregation problems that prevent blood clotting mechanisms.	Autoimmune hemolytic anemia may possibly be inherited. Hemophilia B is inherited as a sex-linked recessive trait. Thrombasthenic thrombapathia is inherited as an autosomal dominant trait. von Willebrand's disease is inherited differently in various breeds. It is an autosomal recessive trait in Scottish Terriers.
Bone and joint disorders: 1. Achondroplasia 2. Craniomandibular osteopathy (also called lion jaw, westy jaw, or Scotty jaw)	1. Short curved legs. 2. Excessive bone development on the bottom jaw, usually seen at 4 to 7 months of age, accompanied by discomfort when chewing.	Autosomal recessive inheritances.
Cancer: 1. Lymphosarcoma 2. Squamous cell carcinoma 3. Melanoma	Malignant forms of cancer that cause overall debilitation and eventual death.	
Ears: deafness	Inability to hear.	Can be inherited.
Eyes: 1. Cataracts 2. Luxated lens 3. Progressive retinal atrophy 4. Persistent pupillary membranes	1. Lens opacity (cloudiness) and eventual blindness. 2. Displacement of the lens from its normal position, causing visual impairment. 3. Degeneration of the retina that progresses to blindness. 4. Persistent blood vessel remnants in the anterior chamber of the eye that may cause visual impairment.	Progressive retinal atrophy is inherited in an autosomal recessive manner.
Urogenital: uterine inertia, dystocia	Difficulty giving birth due to uterine smooth muscle fatigue and anatomical conformation of the dam (small pelvic area) and pup (large head size).	
Central nervous system: Scotty cramp (also called Scotch cramp or recurrent tetany).	Muscular hypertension brought on by excitement or exertion, in which the hind legs are unable to move or are flexed against the body, the back is arched and the dog has a stiff gait, skips, or is unable to stand. Onset can be as early as 6 weeks of age and most affected animals show symptoms by 1 year of age, although some can show symptoms as late as 3 years of age.	Studies suggest Scotty cramp is an autosomal recessive disorder.

*Recessive inheritance means both parents must be carriers of the disorder for it to be expressed in the offspring. Dominant inheritance means only one parent needs to be a carrier of the disorder for some of the offspring to be affected.
Sex-linked inheritance means that the disorder is linked to a chromosome also associated with determining the animal's sex (X or Y).
Autosomal inheritance means the disorder is carried on any chromosome other than the sex chromosomes.

Step One—Controlling Your Scottish Terrier on the Table

An obedient dog is a prerequisite to good grooming. If Scotty is not well-trained, you will not be in full control of the grooming session and that can lead to some clumsy, even dangerous, situations. The key to success is to be gentle and patient, yet firm. Start by standing Scotty on the grooming table and holding him lightly with your hand between his rear legs. (There should always be a rubber nonslip mat on the table top.) If he tries to move or sit down, apply gentle pressure to bring him back to the right position. Don't try to position him by lifting him under the stomach. This will cause him to hunch up. Reassure Scotty by talking to him in a happy voice and petting him. Make this first training session short, no longer than five minutes. When you are finished, praise Scotty for his cooperation, consider giving him a small food reward, and set him on the floor. This is your way of telling him that his time on the table has ended. If desired, you can repeat these mini-training sessions two or three times a day until Scotty feels comfortable and happy standing on the table.

Step Two—Handling, Brushing, and Combing

Once Scotty is accustomed to standing on the grooming table and remains standing without attempting to jump off of the table, you can begin training him to be handled. Begin by gently lifting and holding each foot for a few seconds. As he becomes used to having his feet handled, you can hold each foot for longer periods of time and handle each toe individually (as you will have to do later when you trim his nails). Gently handle Scotty's ears, face, body, and tail. When he accepts your handling calmly and remains standing on the table, you can introduce him to a soft brush or a gentle comb. At this point it really does not matter if you comb out any dirt or tangles. The idea is to let Scotty become accustomed to a strange or unfamiliar object touching his body. Simply place the brush or comb lightly on his back and sides and then begin to gently slide it along the surface of the coat. Don't worry about the face and ears right now. If Scotty seems to enjoy the massage, continue for a few more minutes. Be sure to stop before he tires of it. If

A mirror on the wall is helpful in allowing you to compare both sides of your pet while you work, so that your Scottish Terrier is groomed the same on both sides. Never leave your Scottish Terrier unsupervised on the grooming table.

GROOMING

you are training a young puppy, remember that puppies bore easily so you may want to limit this session to three to five minutes.

Step Three—Working Around the Face and Toenails

You may begin working on and around Scotty's face once he has learned to accept having his body brushed and combed. Be sure Scotty is very well-trained before you work with scissors or other objects near his eyes and ears. Start by scratching the ears, inside and out, and under the chin. Take a soft cotton cloth or tissue and gently wipe the corners of the eyes and then the corners of the nostrils. Lift the lips and open Scotty's mouth. Try to perform these activities in the same order. Make them a brief, but repetitive, routine followed by plenty of praise. Continue to handle and lift the feet. If all is proceeding well, now is a good time to pretend to use the nail clippers. Let Scotty become familiar with the sound the clippers make, set them on the nails, but do not cut the nails.

Step Four—Detail Work

It will take many sessions before Scotty has completely adapted to the routine of standing on the grooming table and being handled and

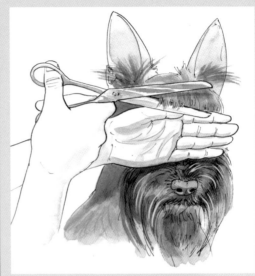

Be very careful with sharp objects around your Scottish Terrier's face. To prevent accidental injury, be sure to protect your pet's eyes whenever you use scissors or other grooming tools in the facial area.

brushed. When you are both ready (and not before!), you can begin the detail work of thinning and trimming the coat, and trimming the face, ears, tail, and feet. You can learn many tricks of the trade from other Scottish Terrier owners or professional dog groomers. The more you practice, the more skilled you will become, and the better Scotty will look!

SCOTTISH TERRIERS DO IT ALL

As you well know by now from your personal experiences with your own Scottish Terrier, these dogs are proud, brave, bossy, independent, tenacious, sometimes obstinate, and have a true sense of humor. They are also extremely bright and energetic and there is no limit to the things they can learn and do.

Dog Shows

Dog shows are a lot of fun for both exhibitors and observers. Dogs are judged on how closely they come to the ideal standard for conformation for their breeds. If Scotty is handsome enough to compete against the best of his breed, consider joining a Scottish Terrier club, as well as a local kennel club. These clubs can provide you with information on show dates and locations, judges, professional handlers, canine activities, and even offer handling classes to teach you and your dog the ropes. Dog clubs also organize fun matches—dog shows where you can practice and perfect what you've learned before you participate in an all-breed or specialty (one breed only, in your case, Scottish Terriers) show.

When a Scottish Terrier is having fun, its enthusiasm is contagious!

Fun Matches

You can prepare yourself and your puppy for a future in the conformation ring by attending fun matches. Fun matches are just that—fun! They are hosted by American Kennel Club approved breed clubs and conducted according to American Kennel Club show rules. Only purebred, AKC registered dogs may participate. However, fun matches do not count toward points for a championship, and dogs that have won points toward a championship do not compete. Judges at fun matches may be official AKC judges, or a knowledgeable dog breeder or handler selected by the hosting club. Fun matches are a great way for you and your puppy to practice all aspects of a real dog show, from traveling and grooming, to exhibiting and winning!

Specialty Shows

Under the American Kennel Club show regulations, there are two types of conformation shows: specialty shows and all-breed shows. Dogs are judged according to their breed standard, and by a process of elimination, one dog is selected as Best of Breed.

A specialty show is limited to a designated breed or grouping of breeds. For example, the Scottish Terrier Club of America holds an annual show for Scottish Terriers only. The show is held under AKC rules by the individual breed clubs.

The Scottish Terrier Club of America is responsible for maintaining the official standards of the breed. If there are any changes or revisions to be made, the club must approve them before submitting them for final approval to the AKC.

Scottish Terriers are assigned points, based on their conformation, as follows:

Scale of Points

Skull	5
Muzzle	5
Eyes	5
Ears	10
Neck	5
Chest	5
Body	15
Legs and feet	10
Tail	5
Coat	15
Size	10
General appearance	10
Total	**100**

Scottish Terriers are penalized for a soft or curly coat; round, protruding or light eyes; overshot or undershot jaws; obvious oversize or undersize; shyness or timidity; upright shoulders; lack of reach in front or drive in rear; stiff or stilted movements; movement too wide or too close in rear; too narrow in front or rear; out at the elbow; lack of bone and substance; low set tail; lack of pigment in the nose; coarse head; and failure to show with head and tail up. In addition, the rules state: "No judge should put to winners or best of breed any Scottish Terrier not showing real terrier character in the ring."

In order to become a champion, a Scottish Terrier must win a minimum of 15 points by competing in formal, American Kennel Club sanctioned, licensed events. The points must be accumulated as major wins under different judges.

All-breed Shows

As the name implies, all-breed shows are for all breeds. Judging is conducted according to AKC rules. In addition to Best of Breed winners, Open Shows offer the title of Best in Group (for dogs considered to be the best representative of their group) and Best in Show (for the dog selected as the best representative of its breed and group, compared to all other dogs of other breeds and groups).

Most dogs competing in Specialty or Open Shows are competing for points toward their championship. A dog can earn from one to five points at a show. The number of points available depends upon the number of entries. Wins of three, four, or five points are called "majors." The fifteen points required for a championship title must be won under at least three different judges and include two majors won under two different judges.

Different Classes

There are five different classes in which a dog can compete for championship points and the classes are divided by sex:

✔ Puppy class (divided into 6 to 9 months of age and 9 to 12 months of age)
✔ Novice
✔ Bred by exhibitor
✔ American bred
✔ Open

Male dogs are judged first in this order: Puppy dogs, Novice dogs, Bred by exhibitor dogs, American bred dogs, and Open dogs. The first place winners in each class return to the showring to compete against each other in what is called the Winners Class. The dog selected as the best male in the Winners Class is the Winners Dog. This is the dog that will win the championship points in the show. The male that placed second to the Winners Dog in his original class (that is, Puppy, Novice, Bred by exhibitor, American bred, or Open) is then brought in to join the Winners Class and compete against the remaining four dogs in the class. The dog that wins second place winner in the Winners Class is the Reserve Winners Dog. If, for any reason, the AKC disallows the championship points to the Winners Dog, the Reserve Winners Dog will receive the points. The same procedure is then followed, in the same order, for the females, and the Winners Bitch (who also wins championship points) and Reserve Winners Bitch are selected.

Best of Breed

The Winners Dog and Winners Bitch then join a class called the Best of Breed. In this class are entered dogs and bitches that have already won their championship titles. The judge selects either the Winners Dog or the Winners Bitch to be Best of Winners and finishes the judging by selecting from the group an animal to be Best of Breed. If the Best of Breed winner is a male, the judge selects the best bitch to be Best of Opposite Sex to the Best of Winners. If the Best of Breed winner is a female, the judge selects a male for Best of Opposite Sex to the Best of Winners.

At an all-breed show, judging takes place for each breed, then each Best of Breed winner competes in its breed group. The seven breed groups are:
✔ Sporting group
✔ Hound group
✔ Working group
✔ Terrier group
✔ Toy group
✔ Non-sporting group
✔ Herding group

The first place winners of each breed group then compete against each other for the coveted title of "Best in Show."

Obedience Trials

In these competitions, it's intelligence that counts. Dogs are put through a series of exercises and commands and judged according to how well they perform. Each dog starts out with 200 points. Points are deducted throughout the trials for lack of attention, nonperformance, barking, or slowness.

Obedience trials are divided into three levels increasing in difficulty:
✔ Novice—Companion Dog (C.D.)
✔ Open—Companion Dog Excellent (C.D.X.)
✔ Utility—Utility Dog (U.D.)

To earn a C.D. title, the dog must be able to perform six exercises: heel on leash, stand for examination, heel free, recall, long sit, and long down. To earn a C.D.X. title the dog must be

Playful, intelligent, and devoted—Scotties have earned their place in the public's heart.

able to heel free, drop on recall, retrieve on flat, retrieve over the high jump, broad jump, long sit, and long down. To earn a U.D., the dog must be able to respond to signal exercise, scent discrimination tests, directed retrieve, directed jumping, and group examination. The dog must earn three legs to earn its title. To receive a leg the dog must earn at least 170 points out of a possible perfect score of 200 and receive more than 50 percent on each exercise.

Agility Competitions

Agility competitions are lots of fun and extremely popular. These are fast-paced, challenging events in which dogs compete in obstacle courses, jump over objects, teeter on seesaws, cross bridges, run through tunnels, and weave through poles. The events are timed and are very exciting. Titles that can be earned, in increasing level of difficulty, are: Novice Agility (NA), Open Agility (OA), Agility Excellent (AX), and Master Agility Excellent (MX).

Games

Scottish Terriers enjoy all kinds of games, from hide-and-seek, to Flyball, to fetch, to Frisbee. And although Scottish Terriers can retrieve, they may not always be willing to relinquish the object! There is no limit to the games and activities a Scottish Terrier is capable of learning when given the opportunity. Whether he is in the showring or the backyard, Scotty will always be a loyal companion, trying his very best to please you. And that's more rewarding than any trophy!

INFORMATION

Kennel and Breed Clubs

American Kennel Club (AKC) Registrations
5580 Centerview Drive
Raleigh, NC 27606-3390
(919) 233-9767
Website: *www.akc.org*

The Canadian Kennel Club
89 Skyway Avenue, Suite 100
Etobicoke, Ontario, Canada
M9W6R4
(416) 675-5511

Federation Cynologique Internationale
Secretariat General de la FCA
Place Albert 1er, 13
B-6530 Thuin, Belgium
Website: *www.fci.be/english*

The Kennel Club
1-4 Clargis Street, Picadilly
London W7Y 8AB England

The Scottish Terrier Club of America (SCTA)
Corresponding Secretary, Susan Clarkson
136 Clunie Drive
Sacramento, CA 95864
(916) 483-9069

States Kennel Club
1007 W. Pine Street
Hattieburg, MS 39401
(601) 583-8345

United Kennel Club (UKC)
100 East Kilgore Road
Kalamazoo, MI 49001-5598
(616) 343-9020

United States Dog Agility Association
P.O. Box 850955
Richardson, TX 75085-8955

(972) 231-9700
Fax: (214) 503-0161
Website: *www.usdaa.com*
E-mail: *info@usdaa.com*

Health Related Associations and Foundations

American Society for the Prevention of Cruelty
    to Animals (ASPCA)
424 East 92nd Street
New York, NY 10128-6804
(212) 876-7700
Website: *www.aspca.org*

American Veterinary Medical Association (AVMA)
930 North Meacham Road
Schaumberg, IL 60173
Website: *www.avma.org*

Canine Eye Registration Foundation (CERF)
South Campus Court, Building C
West Lafayette, IN 47907

National Animal Poison Control Center (NAPCC)
Animal Product Safety Service
1717 South Philo Road, Suite 36
Urbana, IL 61802
(888) 4ANI-HELP
(888) 426-4435
(900) 680-0000
(Consultation fees apply; call for details.)
Website: *www.napcc.aspca.org*

Orthopedic Foundation for Animals (OFA)
2300 Nifong Boulevard
Columbia, MO 65201
Website: *www.prodogs.com*

Therapy Dogs International
P.O. Box 2796
Cheyenne, WY 82203

Scottish Terriers are protective, brave, and loyal.

Lost Pet Registries

The American Kennel Club (AKC)
AKC Companion Recovery
5580 Centerview Drive, Suite 250
Raleigh, NC 27606-3394
(800) 252-7894
Website: www.akc.org/car.htm
E-mail: found@akc.org

Home Again Microchip Service
(800) LONELY-ONE

National Dog Registry (NDR)
P.O. Box 118
Woodstock, NY 12498-0116
(800) 637-3647

Petfinders
368 High Street
Athol, NY 12810
(800) 223-4747

Tattoo-A-Pet
1625 Emmons Avenue
Brooklyn, NY 11235
(800) TATTOOS

Periodicals

The American Kennel Club Gazette
51 Madison Avenue
New York, NY 10010

Dog Fancy
Subscription Division
P.O. Box 53264
Boulder, CO 80323-3264
(303) 786-7306/666-8504
Website: www.dogfancy.com

Dogs USA Annual
P.O. Box 55811
Boulder, CO 80322-5811
(303) 786-7652

Dog World
29 North Whacker Drive
Chicago, IL 60606
(312) 726-2802

Books

The Complete Dog Book. Official Publication of
the American Kennel Club. New York, NY:
Howell Book House, 1992.
Cooke, Cindy. *The New Scottish Terrier.* New
York, NY: Howell Book House, 1996.
Ewing, Fayette C. *The Book of the Scottish
Terrier.* New York, NY: Orange Judd
Publishing Company, Inc., 1952.
Marvin, John T. *The New Complete Scottish
Terrier.* New York, NY: Howell Book House,
1982.

Important Note

This pet owner's manual tells the reader
how to buy or adopt, and care for a Scottish
Terrier. The author and publisher consider it
important to point out that the advice given
in the book is meant primarily for normally
developed dogs of excellent physical health
and good character.

Anyone who adopts a fully-grown dog
should be aware that the animal has already
formed its basic impressions of human
beings. The new owner should watch the animal carefully, including its behavior toward
humans, and should meet the previous
owner.

Caution is further advised in the association of children with dogs, in meeting with
other dogs, and in exercising the dog without
a leash.

Even well-behaved and carefully supervised dogs sometimes do damage to someone
else's property or cause accidents. It is there-
fore in the owner's interest to be adequately
insured against such eventualities, and we
strongly urge all dog owners to purchase a
liability policy that covers their dog.

About the Author

Sharon Vanderlip, D.V.M., has provided veterinary care to domestic and exotic animal species for more than 20 years. She has written books and articles in scientific and lay publications. Dr. Vanderlip served as the Associate Director of Veterinary Services for the University of California at San Diego School of Medicine, has worked on collaborative projects with the Zoological Society of San Diego, and has had her own veterinary practice. She is the former Chief of Veterinary Services for the National Aeronautics and Space Administration (NASA), and is a consultant in reproductive medicine and surgery for various research and wildlife projects, including the Endangered Red Wolf project. Dr. Vanderlip has lectured at kennel clubs and veterinary associations throughout America and Europe on topics in canine medicine, and is the recipient of various awards for her writing and dedication to animal health.

Acknowledgments

I would like to thank my husband, Jack Vanderlip, D.V.M., for his invaluable help as an expert consultant and for critically reviewing the final manuscript.

His cheerful disposition, ideas, enthusiasm, and continued interest in my projects are greatly appreciated. I would also like to thank editor Mark Miele of Barron's Educational Series, Inc., whose time and assistance contributed significantly to the quality of the manuscript.

Photo Credits

Kent and Donna Dannen: pages 3, 5, 21, 85; Norvia Behling: pages 4, 9 bottom, 13, 16 left, 17 top, 17 bottom, 20, 24 top, 24 bottom left, 24 bottom right, 25 bottom left, 29, 32, 49, 52, 53 top, 53 bottom, 56 top right, 56 bottom left, 56 bottom right, 57 top right, 57 bottom right, 60, 61, 64 top, 64 bottom, 65 left, 65 right, 68, 69, 72, 73, 76, 84, 88 top left, 88 bottom left, 92; Pets by Paulette: pages 8 top left, 8 bottom right, 9 top, 12, 16 right, 25 top, 28, 33, 44, 56 top left, 57 top left, 57 bottom left, 80, 88 bottom right, 89 top, 89 bottom; Tara Darling: pages 8 top right, 8 bottom left, 25 bottom right, 37, 41, 45, 48, 88 top right.

Cover Credits

Kent and Donna Dannen.

All inquiries should be addressed to:
Barron's Educational Series, Inc.
250 Wireless Boulevard
Hauppauge, New York 11788
http://www.barronseduc.com

ISBN-13: 978-0-7641-1639-1
ISBN-10: 0-7641-1639-8

Library of Congress Catalog Card No. 00-052906

Library of Congress Cataloging-in-Publication Data
Vanderlip, Sharon Lynn.
    Scottish terriers : a complete pet owner's manual: everything about purchase, care, nutrition, behavior, and training / Sharon Vanderlip.
        p. cm.
    Includes bibliographical references (p.).
    ISBN 0-7641-1639-8 (alk. paper)
    1. Scottish terrier. I. Title.
SF429.S4 V36 2001
636.755—cd21   00-052906

Printed in China